The Trial and Death
of
Socrates

PLATO

The Trial and Death
of
Socrates

Euthyphro
Apology
Crito
Death Scene from *Phaedo*

Translated by
G. M. A. GRUBE

HACKETT PUBLISHING COMPANY, INC.

ISBN: 0-915144-15-8

Library of Congress Catalog Card Number: 75-33058

second edition, sixth printing, 1985

For further information address Hackett Publishing Company,
Inc., Box 44937, Indianapolis, Indiana 46204

Printed in the United States of America

Cover design by Richard L. Listenberger

CONTENTS

G. M. A. Grube and the publisher acknowledge
with appreciation the extensive help of Richard
Hogan and Donald J. Zeyl in correcting
and improving the second edition of
The Trial & Death of Socrates.

INTRODUCTION

At the time of his trial and execution in 399 B.C., Socrates was seventy years of age. He had lived through the Periclean Age when Athens was at the pinnacle of her imperial power and her cultural ascendancy, then through twenty-five years of war with Sparta and the final defeat of Athens in 404, the oligarchic revolution that followed, and, finally, the restoration of democracy. For most of this time he was a well-known character, expounding his philosophy of life in the streets of Athens to anyone who cared to listen. His "mission," which he explains in the *Apology,* was to expose the ignorance of those who thought themselves wise and to try to convince his fellow-citizens that every man is responsible for his own moral attitudes. The early dialogues of Plato, of which the *Euthyphro* is a good example, show him seeking to define ethical terms and asking awkward questions. There is no reason to suppose that these questions were restricted to the life of the individual. Indeed, if he questioned the basic principles of democracy and adopted towards it anything like the attitude Plato attributes to him, it is no wonder the restored democracy should consider him to have a bad influence on the young.

With the development of democracy and in the intellectual ferment of the fifth century, a need was felt for higher education. To satisfy it, there arose a number of travelling teachers who were called the Sophists. All of them taught rhetoric, the art of public speaking, which was a powerful weapon since all the important decisions were taken by the assemblies of adult male citizens or in the courts with very large juries. Not surprisingly, Socrates was often confused with these Sophists in the public mind, for both of them were apt to question established and inherited values. But their differences were vital: the Sophists professed to put men on the road to success, whereas Socrates disclaimed that he taught anything; his conversations aimed at discovering the truth, at acquiring that knowledge and understanding of life and its values that he thought was the very basis of the good life and of philosophy, to him a moral as well as an intellectual pursuit. Hence his celebrated paradox that virtue is knowledge and that when men do wrong it is only because they do not *know* any better. We are often told

1

that in this theory Socrates ignored the will, but that is in part a misconception. The aim is not to choose the right but to become the sort of person who *cannot* choose the wrong and who no longer has any choice in the matter. This is what he sometimes expresses as becoming like a god, for the gods, as he puts it in the *Euthyphro* (10d), love the right because it is right; they cannot do otherwise and no longer have any choice at all, and they cannot be the cause of evil.

The translations in this volume give the full Platonic account of the drama of Socrates' trial and death. The references to the coming trial and its charges in the *Euthyphro* are a kind of introduction to this drama. The *Apology* is Plato's version of Socrates' speech to the jury in his own defence. In the *Crito* we find Socrates refusing to save his life by escaping into exile. The *Phaedo* gives an account of his discussion with his friends in prison on the last day of his life, mostly on the question of the immortality of the soul. It is a long and philosophically important dialogue which cannot adequately be dealt with here; it requires separate treatment. I have however included the last part of it, the death scene, in which we see Socrates drinking the hemlock, the last act of the whole Socratic tragedy.

The influence of Socrates on his contemporaries can hardly be exaggerated, especially on Plato but not on Plato alone, for a number of authors wrote on Socrates in the early fourth century B.C. And his influence on later philosophers, largely through Plato, was also very great. This impact, on his contemporaries at least, was due not only to his theories but in large measure to his character and personality, that serenely self-confident personality which emerges so vividly from Plato's writings, and in particular from his account of Socrates' trial, imprisonment and execution.

NOTE: With few exceptions, this translation follows Burnet's Oxford text.

EUTHYPHRO

Euthyphro is surprised to meet Socrates near the king-archon's court, for Socrates is not the kind of man to have business with courts of justice. Socrates explains that he is under indictment by one Meletus for corrupting the young and for not believing in the gods in whom the city believes. After a brief discussion of this, Socrates inquires about Euthyphro's business at court and is told that he is prosecuting his own father for the murder of a laborer who is himself a murderer. His family and friends believe his course of action to be impious, but Euthyphro explains that in this they are mistaken and reveal their ignorance of the nature of piety. This naturally leads Socrates to ask, What is piety? and the rest of the dialogue is devoted to a search for a definition of piety, illustrating the Socratic search for universal definitions of ethical terms, to which a number of early Platonic dialogues are devoted. As usual, no definition is found that satisfies Socrates.

The Greek term hosion *means, in the first instance, the knowledge of the proper ritual in prayer and sacrifice, and of course its performance (as Euthyphro himself defines it in 14b). But obviously Euthyphro uses it in the much wider sense of pious conduct generally (e.g., his own) and in that sense the word is practically equivalent to righteousness (the justice of the* Republic*), the transition being by way of conduct pleasing to the gods.*

Besides being an excellent example of the early, so-called Socratic dialogues, Euthyphro *contains several passages with important philosophical implications. These include those in which Socrates speaks of the one Form, presented by all the actions that we call pious (5d), as well as the one in which we are told that the gods love what is pious because it is pious, it is not pious because the gods love it (10d). Another passage clarifies the difference between genus and species (11e). The implications are discussed in the notes on those passages.*

2   EUTHYPHRO:[1] What's new, Socrates, to make you leave your usual
     haunts in the Lyceum and spend your time here by the king-archon's
     court? Surely you are not prosecuting anyone before the king-archon as
     I am?

     SOCRATES: The Athenians do not call this a prosecution but an indict-
     ment, Euthyphro.

b   E: What is this you say? Someone must have indicted you, for
     you are not going to tell me that you have indicted someone else.

         S: No indeed.

         E: But someone else has indicted you?

         S: Quite so.

         E: Who is he?

         S: I do not really know him myself, Euthyphro. He is apparently
     young and unknown. They call him Meletus, I believe. He belongs to
     the Pitthean deme, if you know anyone from that deme called Meletus,
     with long hair, not much of a beard, and a rather aquiline nose.

         E: I don't know him, Socrates. What charge does he bring against
     you?

c   S: What charge? A not ignoble one I think, for it is no small thing
     for a young man to have knowledge of such an important subject. He
     says he knows how our young men are corrupted and who corrupts
     them. He is likely to be wise, and when he sees my ignorance corrupt-
     ing his contemporaries, he proceeds to accuse me to the city as to their

d   mother. I think he is the only one of our public men to start out the
     right way, for it is right to care first that the young should be as good as
     possible, just as a good farmer is likely to take care of the young plants
     first, and of the others later. So, too, Meletus first gets rid of us who

3   corrupt the young shoots, as he says, and then afterwards he will
     obviously take care of the older ones and become a source of great
     blessings for the city, as seems likely to happen to one who started out
     this way.

         E: I could wish this were true, Socrates, but I fear the opposite
     may happen. He seems to me to start out by harming the very heart of
     the city by attempting to wrong you. Tell me, what does he say you do
     to corrupt the young?

---

1. We know nothing about Euthyphro except what we can gather from this dialogue. He is obviously a professional priest who considers himself an expert on ritual
and on piety generally, and, it seems, is generally so considered. One Euthyphro is
mentioned in Plato's *Cratylus* (396d) who is given to *enthousiasmos,* inspiration or possession, but we cannot be sure that it is the same person.

S: Strange things, to hear him tell it, for he says that I am a maker   b
of gods, and on the ground that I create new gods while not believing in
the old gods, he has indicted me for their sake, as he puts it.

E: I understand, Socrates. This is because you say that the divine
sign keeps coming to you.[2] So he has written this indictment against
you as one who makes innovations in religious matters, and he comes
to court to slander you, knowing that such things are easily misrepre-
sented to the crowd. The same is true in my case. Whenever I speak of   c
divine matters in the assembly and foretell the future, they laugh me
down as if I were crazy; and yet I have foretold nothing that did not
happen. Nevertheless, they envy all of us who do this. One need not
worry about them, but meet them head-on.

S: My dear Euthyphro, to be laughed at does not matter perhaps,
for the Athenians do not mind anyone they think clever, as long as he
does not teach his own wisdom, but if they think that he makes others
to be like himself they get angry, whether through envy, as you say, or   d
for some other reason.

E: I have certainly no desire to test their feelings towards me in
this matter.

S: Perhaps you seem to make yourself but rarely available, and
not to be willing to teach your own wisdom, but I'm afraid that my lik-
ing for people makes them think that I pour out to anybody anything I
have to say, not only without charging a fee but even glad to reward
anyone who is willing to listen. If then they were intending to laugh at
me, as you say they laugh at you, there would be nothing unpleasant in   e
their spending their time in court laughing and jesting, but if they are
going to be serious, the outcome is not clear except to you prophets.

E: Perhaps it will come to nothing, Socrates, and you will fight
your case as you think best, as I think I will mine.

S: What is your case, Euthyphro? Are you the defendant or the
prosecutor?

E: The prosecutor.

S: Whom do you prosecute?

E: One whom I am thought crazy to prosecute.   4

S: Are you pursuing someone who will easily escape you?

---

2. In Plato, Socrates always speaks of his divine sign or voice as intervening to
prevent him from doing or saying something (e.g., *Apology* 31d), but never positively.
The popular view was that it enabled him to foretell the future, and Euthyphro here
represents that view. Note, however, that Socrates dissociates himself from "you
prophets" (3e).

E: Far from it, for he is quite old.

S: Who is it?

E: My father.

S: My dear sir! Your own father?

E: Certainly.

S: What is the charge? What is the case about?

E: Murder, Socrates.

S: Good heavens! Certainly, Euthyphro, most men would not
b   know how they could do this and be right. It is not the part of anyone to
do this, but of one who is far advanced in wisdom.

E: Yes, by Zeus, Socrates, that is so.

S: Is then the man your father killed one of your relatives? Or is
that obvious, for you would not prosecute your father for the murder of
a stranger.

E: It is ridiculous, Socrates, for you to think that it makes any
difference whether the victim is a stranger or a relative. One should
only watch whether the killer acted justly or not; if he acted justly, let
c   him go, but if not, one should prosecute, even if the killer shares your
hearth and table. The pollution is the same if you knowingly keep company with such a man and do not cleanse yourself and him by bringing
him to justice. The victim was a dependent of mine, and when we were
farming in Naxos he was a servant of ours. He killed one of our household slaves in drunken anger, so my father bound him hand and foot
and threw him in a ditch, then sent a man here to enquire from the
d   priest what should be done. During that time he gave no thought or
care to the bound man, as being a killer, and it was no matter if he
died, which he did. Hunger and cold and his bonds caused his death
before the messenger came back from the seer. Both my father and my
other relatives are angry that I am prosecuting my father for murder on
behalf of a murderer when he hadn't even killed him, they say, and
even if he had, the dead man does not deserve a thought, since he was a
e   killer. For, they say, it is impious for a son to prosecute his father for
murder. But their ideas of the divine attitude to piety and impiety are
wrong, Socrates.

S: Whereas, by Zeus, Euthyphro, you think that your knowledge
of the divine, and of piety and impiety, is so accurate that, when those
things happened as you say, you have no fear of having acted impiously
in bringing your father to trial?

E: I should be of no use, Socrates, and Euthyphro would not be
5   superior to the majority of men, if I did not have accurate knowledge of
all such things.

S: It is indeed most important, my admirable Euthyphro, that I should become your pupil, and as regards this indictment challenge Meletus about these very things and say to him: that in the past too I considered knowledge about the divine to be most important, and that now that he says that I am guilty of improvising and innovating about the gods I have become your pupil. I would say to him: "If, Meletus, you agree that Euthyphro is wise in these matters, consider me, too, to have the right beliefs and do not bring me to trial. If you do not think so, then prosecute that teacher of mine, not me, for corrupting the older men, me and his own father, by teaching me and by exhorting and punishing him." If he is not convinced, and does not discharge me or indict you instead of me, I shall repeat the same challenge in court.

E: Yes, by Zeus, Socrates, and, if he should try to indict me, I think I would find his weak spots and the talk in court would be about him rather than about me.

S: It is because I realize this that I am eager to become your pupil, my dear friend. I know that other people as well as this Meletus do not even seem to notice you, whereas he sees me so sharply and clearly that he indicts me for ungodliness. So tell me now, by Zeus, what you just now maintained you clearly knew: what kind of thing do you say that godliness and ungodliness are, both as regards murder and other things; or is the pious not the same and alike in every action, and the impious the opposite of all that is pious and like itself, and everything that is to be impious presents us with one form[3] or appearance in so far as it is impious?

E: Most certainly, Socrates.

S: Tell me then, what is the pious, and what the impious, do you say?

E: I say that the pious is to do what I am doing now, to prosecute the wrongdoer, be it about murder or temple robbery or anything else, whether the wrongdoer is your father or your mother or anyone else; not to prosecute is impious. And observe, Socrates, that I can quote the law as a great proof that this is so. I have already said to others that

---

3. This is the kind of passage that makes it easier for us to follow the transition from Socrates' universal definitions to the Platonic theory of separately existent eternal universal Forms. The words *eidos* and *idea,* the technical terms for the Platonic Forms, commonly mean physical stature or bodily appearance. As we apply a common epithet, in this case pious, to different actions or things, these must have a common characteristic, present a common appearance or form, to justify the use of the same term, but in the early dialogues, as here, it seems to be thought of as immanent in the particulars and without separate existence. The same is true of 6d where the word "Form" is also used.

such actions are right, not to favour the ungodly, whoever they are. These people themselves believe that Zeus is the best and most just of
6   the gods, yet they agree that he bound his father because he unjustly swallowed his sons, and that he in turn castrated his father for similar reasons. But they are angry with me because I am prosecuting my father for his wrongdoing. They contradict themselves in what they say about the gods and about me.

S: Indeed, Euthyphro, this is the reason why I am a defendant in the case, because I find it hard to accept things like that being said about the gods, and it is likely to be the reason why I shall be told I do wrong. Now, however, if you, who have full knowledge of such things,
b   share their opinions, then we must agree with them too, it would seem. For what are we to say, we who agree that we ourselves have no knowledge of them? Tell me, by the god of friendship, do you really believe these things are true?

E: Yes, Socrates, and so are even more surprising things, of which the majority has no knowledge.

S: And do you believe that there really is war among the gods, and terrible enmities and battles, and other such things as are told by
c   the poets, and other sacred stories such as are embroidered by good writers and by representations of which the robe of the goddess is adorned when it is carried up to the Acropolis? Are we to say these things are true, Euthyphro?

E: Not only these, Socrates, but, as I was saying just now, I will, if you wish, relate many other things about the gods which I know will amaze you.

S: I should not be surprised, but you will tell me these at leisure some other time. For now, try to tell me more clearly what I was asking
d   just now, for, my friend, you did not teach me adequately when I asked you what the pious was, but you told me that what you are doing now, prosecuting your father for murder, is pious.

E: And I told the truth, Socrates.

S: Perhaps. You agree, however, that there are many other pious actions.

E: There are.

S: Bear in mind then that I did not bid you tell me one or two of the many pious actions but that form itself that makes all pious actions pious, for you agreed that all impious actions are impious and all pious
e   actions pious through one form, or don't you remember?

E: I do.

S: Tell me then what this form itself is, so that I may look upon it, and using it as a model, say that any action of yours or another's that is of that kind is pious, and if it is not that it is not.

E: If that is how you want it, Socrates, that is how I will tell you.

S: That is what I want.

E: Well then, what is dear to the gods is pious, what is not is impious. 7

S: Splendid, Euthyphro! You have now answered in the way I wanted. Whether your answer is true I do not know yet, but you will obviously show me that what you say is true.

E: Certainly.

S: Come then, let us examine what we mean. An action or a man dear to the gods is pious, but an action or a man hated by the gods is impious. They are not the same, but quite opposite, the pious and the impious. Is that not so?

E: It is indeed.

S: And that seems to be a good statement?

E: I think so, Socrates. b

S: We have also stated that the gods are in a state of discord, that they are at odds with each other, Euthyphro, and that they are at enmity with each other. Has that, too, been said?

E: It has.

S: What are the subjects of difference that cause hatred and anger? Let us look at it this way. If you and I were to differ about numbers as to which is the greater, would this difference make us enemies and angry with each other, or would we proceed to count and soon resolve our difference about this? c

E: We would certainly do so.

S: Again, if we differed about the larger and the smaller, we would turn to measurement and soon cease to differ.

E: That is so.

S: And about the heavier and the lighter, we would resort to weighing and be reconciled.

E: Of course.

S: What subject of difference would make us angry and hostile to each other if we were unable to come to a decision? Perhaps you do not have an answer ready, but examine as I tell you whether these subjects d are the just and the unjust, the beautiful and the ugly, the good and the bad. Are these not the subjects of difference about which, when we are unable to come to a satisfactory decision, you and I and other men become hostile to each other whenever we do?

E: That is the difference, Socrates, about those subjects.

S: What about the gods, Euthyphro? If indeed they have differences, will it not be about these same subjects?

E: It certainly must be so.

e

S: Then according to your argument, my good Euthyphro, different gods consider different things to be just, beautiful, ugly, good, and bad, for they would not be at odds with one another unless they differed about these subjects, would they?

E: You are right.

S: And they like what each of them considers beautiful, good, and just, and hate the opposites of these?

E: Certainly.

8

S: But you say that the same things are considered just by some gods and unjust by others, and as they dispute about these things they are at odds and at war with each other. Is that not so?

E: It is.

S: The same things then are loved by the gods and hated by the gods, and would be both god-loved and god-hated.

E: It seems likely.

S: And the same things would be both pious and impious, according to this argument?

E: I'm afraid so.

S: So you did not answer my question, you surprising man. I did not ask you what same thing is both pious and impious, and it appears

b

that what is loved by the gods is also hated by them. So it is in no way surprising if your present action, namely punishing your father, may be pleasing to Zeus but displeasing to Kronos and Ouranos, pleasing to Hephaestus but displeasing to Hera, and so with any other gods who differ from each other on this subject.

E: I think, Socrates, that on this subject no gods would differ from one another, that whoever has killed anyone unjustly should pay the penalty.

c

S: Well now, Euthyphro, have you ever heard any man maintaining that one who has killed or done anything else unjustly should not pay the penalty?

E: They never cease to dispute on this subject, both elsewhere and in the courts, for when they have committed many wrongs they do and say anything to avoid the penalty.

S: Do they agree they have done wrong, Euthyphro, and in spite of so agreeing do they nevertheless say they should not be punished?

E: No, they do not agree on that point.

S: So they do not say or do anything. For they do not venture to say this, or dispute that they must not pay the penalty if they have done wrong, but I think they deny doing wrong. Is that not so?   d

E: That is true.

S: Then they do not dispute that the wrongdoer must be punished, but they may disagree as to who the wrongdoer is, what he did and when.

E: You are right.

S: Do not the gods have the same experience, if indeed they are at odds with each other about the just and the unjust, as your argument maintains? Some assert that they wrong one another, while others deny it, but no one among gods or men ventures to say that the wrongdoer   e
must not be punished.

E: Yes, that is true, Socrates, as to the main point.

S: And those who disagree, whether men or gods, dispute about each action, if indeed the gods disagree. Some say it is done justly, others unjustly. Is that not so?

E: Yes, indeed.

S: Come now, my dear Euthyphro, tell me, too, that I may be-   9
come wiser, what proof you have that all the gods consider that man to have been killed unjustly who became a murderer while in your service, was bound by the master of his victim, and died in his bonds before the one who bound him found out from the seers what was to be done with him, and that it is right for a son to denounce and to prosecute his father on behalf of such a man. Come, try to show me a clear sign that all the gods definitely believe this action to be right. If   b
you can give me adequate proof of this, I shall never cease to extol your wisdom.

E: This is perhaps no light task, Socrates, though I could show you very clearly.

S: I understand that you think me more dull-witted than the jury, as you will obviously show them that these actions were unjust and that all the gods hate such actions.

E: I will show it to them clearly, Socrates, if only they will listen to me.

S: They will listen if they think you show them well. But this   c
thought came to me as you were speaking, and I am examining it, say-ing to myself: "If Euthyphro shows me conclusively that all the gods consider such a death unjust, to what greater extent have I learned from him the nature of piety and impiety? This action would then, it seems, be hated by the gods, but the pious and the impious were not thereby

now defined, for what is hated by the gods has also been shown to be loved by them." So I will not insist on this point; let us assume, if you wish, that all the gods consider this unjust and that they all hate it.

d However, is this the correction we are making in our discussion, that what all the gods hate is impious, and what they all love is pious, and that what some gods love and others hate is neither or both? Is that how you now wish us to define piety and impiety?

E: What prevents us from doing so, Socrates?

S: For my part nothing, Euthyphro, but you look whether on your part this proposal will enable you to teach me most easily what you promised.

e E: I would certainly say that the pious is what all the gods love, and the opposite, what all the gods hate, is the impious.

S: Then let us again examine whether that is a sound statement, or do we let it pass, and if one of us, or someone else, merely says that something is so, do we accept that it is so? Or should we examine what the speaker means?

E: We must examine it, but I certainly think that this is now a fine statement.

10 S: We shall soon know better whether it is. Consider this: Is the pious loved by the gods because it is pious, or is it pious because it is loved by the gods?

E: I don't know what you mean, Socrates.

S: I shall try to explain more clearly: we speak of something being carried[4] and something carrying, of something being led and something leading, of something being seen and something seeing, and you understand that these things are all different from one another and how they differ?

E: I think I do.

S: So there is something being loved and something loving, and the loving is a different thing.

---

4. This is the present participle form of the verb *pheromenon*, literally *being-carried*. The following passage is somewhat obscure, especially in translation, but the general meaning is clear. Plato points out that this participle simply indicates the object of an action of carrying, seeing, loving, etc. It follows from the action and adds nothing new, the action being prior to it, not following from it, and a thing is said to be loved because someone loves it, not vice versa. To say therefore that the pious is being loved by the gods says no more than that the gods love it. Euthyphro, however, also agrees that the pious is loved by the gods because of its nature (because it is pious), but the fact of its being loved by the gods does not define that nature, and as a definition is therefore unsatisfactory. It only indicates a quality or affect of the pious, and the pious is therefore still to be defined (11a7).

E: Of course.

S: Tell me then whether that which is being carried is being car-   b
ried because someone carries it or for some other reason.

E: No, that is the reason.

S: And that which is being led is so because someone leads it, and
that which is being seen because someone sees it?

E: Certainly.

S: It is not seen by someone because it is being seen but on the
contrary it is being seen because someone sees it, nor is it because it is
being led that someone leads it but because someone leads it that it is
being led; nor does someone carry an object because it is being carried,
but it is being carried because someone carries it. Is what I want to say
clear, Euthyphro? I want to say this, namely, that if anything comes to   c
be, or is affected, it does not come to be because it is coming to be, but
it is coming to be because it comes to be; nor is it affected because it is
being affected but because something affects it. Or do you not agree?

E: I do.

S: What is being loved is either something that comes to be or
something that is affected by something?

E: Certainly.

S: So it is in the same case as the things just mentioned; it is not
loved by those who love it because it is being loved, but it is being loved
because they love it?

E: Necessarily.

S: What then do we say about the pious, Euthyphro? Surely that   d
it is loved by all the gods, according to what you say?

E: Yes.

S: Is it loved because it is pious, or for some other reason?

E: For no other reason.

S: It is loved then because it is pious, but it is not pious because it
is loved?[5]

---

5. I quote an earlier comment of mine on this passage: ". . . it gives in a nutshell a
point of view from which Plato never departed. Whatever the gods may be, they must
by their very nature love the right because it is right." They have no choice in the matter. "This separation of the dynamic power of the gods from the ultimate reality, this
setting up of absolute values above the gods themselves was not as unnatural to a Greek
as it would be to us. . . . The gods who ruled on Olympus . . . were not creators but
created beings. As in Homer, Zeus must obey the balance of Necessity, so the Platonic
gods must conform to an eternal scale of values. They did not create them, cannot alter
them, cannot indeed wish to do so." *(Plato's Thought,* Indianapolis: Hackett Publishing
Co., 1980, pp. 152-3.)

E: Apparently.

S: And because it is loved by the gods it is being loved and is dear to the gods?

E: Of course.

S: The god-beloved is then not the same as the pious, Euthyphro, nor the pious the same as the god-beloved, as you say it is, but one differs from the other.

e   E: How so, Socrates?

S: Because we agree that the pious is beloved for the reason that it is pious, but it is not pious because it is loved. Is that not so?

E: Yes.

S: And that the god-beloved, on the other hand, is so because it is loved by the gods, by the very fact of being loved, but it is not loved because it is god-beloved.

E: True.

S: But if the god-beloved and the pious were the same, my dear Euthyphro, and the pious were loved because it was pious, then the
11   god-beloved would be loved because it was god-beloved, and if the god-beloved was god-beloved because it was loved by the gods, then the pious would also be pious because it was loved by the gods; but now you see that they are in opposite cases as being altogether different from each other: the one is of a nature to be loved because it is loved, the other is loved because it is of a nature to be loved. I'm afraid, Euthyphro, that when you were asked what piety is, you did not wish to make its nature clear to me, but you told me an affect or quality of it, that the pious has the quality of being loved by all the gods, but you
b   have not yet told me what the pious is. Now, if you will, do not hide things from me but tell me again from the beginning what piety is, whether loved by the gods or having some other quality — we shall not quarrel about that — but be keen to tell me what the pious and the impious are.

E: But Socrates, I have no way of telling you what I have in mind, for whatever proposition we put forward goes around and refuses to stay put where we establish it.

S: Your statements, Euthyphro, seem to belong to my ancestor,
c   Daedalus. If I were stating them and putting them forward, you would perhaps be making fun of me and say that because of my kinship with him my conclusions in discussion run away and will not stay where one puts them. As these propositions are yours, however, we need some other jest, for they will not stay put for you, as you say yourself.

E: I think the same jest will do for our discussion, Socrates, for I am not the one who makes them go round and not remain in the same place; it is you who are the Daedalus; for as far as I am concerned they would remain as they were.

d

S: It looks as if I was cleverer than Daedalus in using my skill, my friend, in so far as he could only cause to move the things he made himself, but I can make other people's move as well as my own. And the smartest part of my skill is that I am clever without wanting to be, for I would rather have your statements to me remain unmoved than possess the wealth of Tantalus as well as the cleverness of Daedalus. But enough of this. Since I think you are making unnecessary difficulties, I am as eager as you are to find a way to teach me about piety, and do not give up before you do. See whether you think all that is pious is of necessity just.

e

E: I think so.

S: And is then all that is just pious? Or is all that is pious just, but not all that is just pious, but some of it is and some is not?

12

E: I do not follow what you are saying, Socrates.

S: Yet you are younger than I by as much as you are wiser. As I say, you are making difficulties because of your wealth of wisdom. Pull yourself together, my dear sir, what I am saying is not difficult to grasp. I am saying the opposite of what the poet said who wrote:
You do not wish to name Zeus, who had done it, and who made all things grow, for where there is fear there is also shame.
I disagree with the poet. Shall I tell you why?

b

E: Please do.

S: I do not think that "where there is fear there is also shame," for I think that many people who fear disease and poverty and many other such things feel fear, but are not ashamed of the things they fear. Do you not think so?

E: I do indeed.

S: But where there is shame there is also fear. For is there anyone who, in feeling shame and embarrassment at anything, does not also at the same time fear and dread a reputation for wickedness?

c

E: He is certainly afraid.

S: It is then not right to say "where there is fear there is also shame," but that where there is shame there is also fear, for fear covers a larger area than shame. Shame is a part of fear just as odd is a part of number, with the result that it is not true that where there is number there is also oddness, but that where there is oddness there is also number. Do you follow me now?

E: Surely.

S: This is the kind of thing I was asking before, whether where
d   there is piety there is also justice, but where there is justice there is not
always piety, for the pious is a part of justice. Shall we say that, or do
you think otherwise?

E: No, but like that, for what you say appears to be right.

S: See what comes next: if the pious is a part of the just, we must,
it seems, find out what part of the just it is. Now if you asked me something of what we mentioned just now, such as what part of number is
the even, and what number that is, I would say it is the number that is
divisible into two equal, not unequal, parts. Or do you not think so?

E: I do.

e   S: Try in this way to tell me what part of the just the pious is, in
order to tell Meletus not to wrong us any more and not to indict me for
ungodliness, since I have learned from you sufficiently what is godly
and pious and what is not.

E: I think, Socrates, that the godly and pious is the part of the just
that is concerned with the care of the gods, while that concerned with
the care of men is the remaining part of justice.

S: You seem to me to put that very well, but I still need a bit of in-
13   formation. I do not know yet what you mean by care, for you do not
mean the care of the gods in the same sense as the care of other things,
as, for example, we say, don't we, that not everyone knows how to care
for horses, but the horse breeder does.

E: Yes, I do mean it that way.

S: So horse breeding is the care of horses.

E: Yes.

S: Nor does everyone know how to care for dogs, but the hunter
does.

E: That is so.

S: So hunting is the care of dogs.

b   E: Yes.

S: And cattle raising is the care of cattle.

E: Quite so.

S: While piety and godliness is the care of the gods, Euthyphro. Is
that what you mean?

E: It is.

S: Now care in each case has the same effect; it aims at the good
and the benefit of the object cared for, as you can see that horses cared

for by horse breeders are benefited and become better. Or do you not think so?

E: I do.

S: So dogs are benefited by dog breeding, cattle by cattle raising, and so with all the others. Or do you think that care aims to harm the   c object of its care?

E: By Zeus, no.

S: It aims to benefit the object of its care?

E: Of course.

S: Is piety then, which is the care of the gods, also to benefit the gods and make them better? Would you agree that when you do something pious you make some one of the gods better?

E: By Zeus, no.

S: Nor do I think that this is what you mean — far from it — but that is why I asked you what you meant by the care of gods, because I did not believe you meant this kind of care.   d

E: Quite right, Socrates, that is not the kind of care I mean.

S: Very well, but what kind of care of the gods would piety be?

E: The kind of care, Socrates, that slaves take of their masters.

S: I understand. It is likely to be a kind of service of the gods.

E: Quite so.

S: Could you tell me to the achievement of what goal service to doctors tends? Is it not, do you think, to achieving health?

E: I think so.

S: What about service to shipbuilders? To what achievement is it   e directed?

E: Clearly, Socrates, to the building of a ship.

S: And service to housebuilders to the building of a house?

E: Yes.

S: Tell me then, my good sir, to the achievement of what aim does service to the gods tend? You obviously know since you say that you, of all men, have the best knowledge of the divine.

E: And I am telling the truth, Socrates.

S: Tell me then, by Zeus, what is that excellent aim that the gods achieve, using us as their servants?

E: Many fine things, Socrates.

S: So do generals, my friend. Nevertheless you could easily tell   14 me their main concern, which is to achieve victory in war, is it not?

E: Of course.

S: The farmers too, I think, achieve many fine things, but the main point of their efforts is to produce food from the earth.

E: Quite so.

S: Well then, how would you sum up the many fine things that the gods achieve?

b
E: I told you a short while ago, Socrates, that it is a considerable task to acquire any precise knowledge of these things, but, to put it simply, I say that if a man knows how to say and do what is pleasing to the gods at prayer and sacrifice, those are pious actions such as preserve both private houses and public affairs of state. The opposite of these pleasing actions are impious and overturn and destroy everything.

c
S: You could tell me in far fewer words, if you were willing, the sum of what I asked, Euthyphro, but you are not keen to teach me, that is clear. You were on the point of doing so, but you turned away. If you had given that answer, I should now have acquired from you sufficient knowledge of the nature of piety. As it is, the lover of inquiry must follow his beloved wherever it may lead him. Once more then, what do you say that piety and the pious are? Are they a knowledge of how to sacrifice and pray?

E: They are.

S: To sacrifice is to make a gift to the gods, whereas to pray is to beg from the gods?

E: Definitely, Socrates.

d
S: It would follow from this statement that piety would be a knowledge of how to give to, and beg from, the gods.

E: You understood what I said very well, Socrates.

S: That is because I am so desirous of your wisdom, and I concentrate my mind on it, so that no word of yours may fall to the ground. But tell me, what is this service to the gods? You say it is to beg from them and to give to them?

E: I do.

S: And to beg correctly would be to ask from them things that we need?

E: What else?

e
S: And to give correctly is to give them what they need from us, for it would not be skillful to bring gifts to anyone that are in no way needed.

E: True, Socrates.

S: Piety would then be a sort of trading skill between gods and men?

E: Trading yes, if you prefer to call it that.

S: I prefer nothing, unless it is true. But tell me, what benefit do the gods derive from the gifts they receive from us? What they give us is obvious to all. There is for us no good that we do not receive from   15 them, but how are they benefited by what they receive from us? Or do we have such an advantage over them in the trade that we receive all our blessings from them and they receive nothing from us?

E: Do you suppose, Socrates, that the gods are benefited by what they receive from us?

S: What could those gifts from us to the gods be, Euthyphro?

E: What else, do you think, than honour, reverence, and what I mentioned just now, gratitude?

S: The pious is then, Euthyphro, pleasing to the gods, but not   b beneficial or dear to them?

E: I think it is of all things most dear to them.

S: So the pious is once again what is dear to the gods.

E: Most certainly.

S: When you say this, will you be surprised if your arguments seem to move about instead of staying put? And will you accuse me of being Daedalus who makes them move, though you are yourself much more skillful than Daedalus and make them go round in a circle? Or do you not realize that our argument has moved around and come again to the same place? You surely remember that earlier the pious and the   c god-beloved were shown not to be the same but different from each other. Or do you not remember?

E: I do.

S: Do you then not realize now that you are saying that what is dear to the gods is the pious? Is this not the same as the god-beloved? Or is it not?

E: It certainly is.

S: Either we were wrong when we agreed before, or, if we were right then, we are wrong now.

E: That seems to be so.

S: So we must investigate again from the beginning what piety is, as I shall not willingly give up before I learn this. Do not think me unworthy, but concentrate your attention and tell the truth. For you   d know it, if any man does, and I must not let you go, like Proteus, before you tell me. If you had no clear knowledge of piety and impiety you would never have ventured to prosecute your old father for murder on behalf of a servant. For fear of the gods you would have been afraid to take the risk lest you should not be acting rightly, and would have been ashamed before men, but now I know well that you believe you have clear knowledge of piety and impiety. So tell me, my good Euthyphro, and do not hide what you think it is.

E: Some other time, Socrates, for I am in a hurry now, and it is time for me to go.

S: What a thing to do, my friend! By going you have cast me down from a great hope I had, that I would learn from you the nature of the pious and the impious and so escape Meletus' indictment by showing him that I had acquired wisdom in divine matters from Euthyphro, and my ignorance would no longer cause me to be careless and inventive about such things, and that I would be better for the rest of my life.

APOLOGY

The Apology[1] *professes to be a record of the actual speech that Socrates delivered in his own defence at the trial. This makes the question of its historicity more acute than in the dialogues in which the conversations themselves are mostly fictional and the question of historicity is concerned only with how far the theories that Socrates is represented as expressing were those of the historical Socrates. Here, however, we are dealing with a speech that Socrates made as a matter of history. How far is Plato's account accurate? We should always remember that the ancients did not expect historical accuracy in the way we do. On the other hand, Plato makes it clear that he was present at the trial (34a, 38b). Moreover, if, as is generally believed, the* Apology *was written not long after the event, many Athenians would remember the actual speech, and it would be a poor way to vindicate the Master, which is the obvious intent, to put a completely different speech into his mouth. Some liberties could no doubt be allowed, but the main arguments and the general tone of the defence must surely be faithful to the original. The beauty of language and style is certainly Plato's, but the serene spiritual and moral beauty of character belongs to Socrates. It is a powerful combination.*

Athenian juries were very large, in this case 501, and they combined the duties of jury and judge as we know them by both convicting and sentencing. Obviously, it would have been virtually impossible for so large a body to discuss various penalties and decide on one. The problem was resolved rather neatly, however, by having the prosecutor, after conviction, assess the penalty he thought appropriate, followed by a counter-assessment by the defendant. The jury would then decide between the two. This procedure generally made for moderation on both sides.

Thus the Apology *is in three parts. The first and major part is the main speech (17a - 35a), followed by the counter-assessment (35a - 38c), and finally, last words to the jury (38c - 42a), both to those who voted for the death sentence and those who voted for acquittal.*

---

1. The word *apology* is a transliteration, not a translation, of the Greek *apologia* which means defence. There is certainly nothing apologetic about the speech.

21

17   I do not know, men of Athens, how my accusers affected you; as for me, I was almost carried away in spite of myself, so persuasively did they speak. And yet, hardly anything of what they said is true. Of the many lies they told, one in particular surprised me, namely that you should be careful not to be deceived by an accomplished speaker like

b   me. That they were not ashamed to be immediately proved wrong by the facts, when I show myself not to be an accomplished speaker at all, that I thought was most shameless on their part — unless indeed they call an accomplished speaker the man who speaks the truth. If they mean that, I would agree that I am an orator, but not after their manner, for indeed, as I say, practically nothing they said was true. From

c   me you will hear the whole truth, though not, by Zeus, gentlemen, expressed in embroidered and stylized phrases like theirs, but things spoken at random and expressed in the first words that come to mind, for I put my trust in the justice of what I say, and let none of you expect anything else. It would not be fitting at my age, as it might be for a young man, to toy with words when I appear before you.

        One thing I do ask and beg of you, gentlemen: if you hear me making my defence in the same kind of language as I am accustomed to use in the market place by the bankers' tables,[2] where many of you have heard me, and elsewhere, do not be surprised or create a disturbance

d   on that account. The position is this: this is my first appearance in a lawcourt, at the age of seventy; I am therefore simply a stranger to the manner of speaking here. Just as if I were really a stranger, you would certainly excuse me if I spoke in that dialect and manner in which I had

18   been brought up, so too my present request seems a just one, for you to pay no attention to my manner of speech — be it better or worse — but to concentrate your attention on whether what I say is just or not, for the excellence of a judge lies in this, as that of a speaker lies in telling the truth.

        It is right for me, gentlemen, to defend myself first against the first lying accusations made against me and my first accusers, and then against the later accusations and the later accusers. There have been

b   many who have accused me to you for many years now, and none of their accusations are true. These I fear much more than I fear Anytus and his friends, though they too are formidable. These earlier ones, however, are more so, gentlemen; they got hold of most of you from childhood, persuaded you and accused me quite falsely, saying that there is a man called Socrates, a wise man, a student of all things in the

c   sky and below the earth, who makes the worse argument the stronger. Those who spread that rumour, gentlemen, are my dangerous

---

2. The bankers or money-changers had their counters in the market place. It seems that this was a favourite place for gossip.

accusers, for their hearers believe that those who study these things do not even believe in the gods. Moreover, these accusers are numerous, and have been at it a long time; also, they spoke to you at an age when you would most readily believe them, some of you being children and adolescents, and they won their case by default, as there was no defence.

What is most absurd in all this is that one cannot even know or mention their names unless one of them is a writer of comedies.[3] d
Those who maliciously and slanderously persuaded you — who also, when persuaded themselves then persuaded others — all those are most difficult to deal with: one cannot bring one of them into court or refute him; one must simply fight with shadows, as it were, in making one's defence, and cross-examine when no one answers. I want you to realize too that my accusers are of two kinds: those who have accused me recently, and the old ones I mention; and to think that I must first defend myself against the latter, for you have also heard e
their accusations first, and to a much greater extent than the more recent.

Very well then. I must surely defend myself and attempt to uproot from your minds in so short a time the slander that has resided there so 19
long. I wish this may happen, if it is in any way better for you and me, and that my defence may be successful, but I think this is very difficult and I am fully aware of how difficult it is. Even so, let the matter proceed as the god may wish, but I must obey the law and make my defence.

Let us then take up the case from its beginning. What is the accusation from which arose the slander in which Meletus trusted when he b
wrote out the charge against me? What did they say when they slandered me? I must, as if they were my actual prosecutors, read the affidavit they would have sworn. It goes something like this: Socrates is guilty of wrongdoing in that he busies himself studying things in the sky and below the earth; he makes the worse into the stronger argument, and he teaches these same things to others. You have seen this yourselves in the comedy of Aristophanes, a Socrates swinging about c
there, saying he was walking on air and talking a lot of other nonsense about things of which I know nothing at all. I do not speak in contempt of such knowledge, if someone is wise in these things — lest Meletus bring more cases against me — but, gentlemen, I have no part in it, and on this point I call upon the majority of you as witnesses. I think it right that all those of you who have heard me conversing, and many of you have, should tell each other if anyone of you has ever heard me dis- d

---

3. This refers in particular to Aristophanes, whose comedy, *The Clouds,* produced in 423 B.C., ridiculed the (imaginary) school of Socrates.

cussing such subjects to any extent at all. From this you will learn that
the other things said about me by the majority are of the same kind.

Not one of them is true. And if you have heard from anyone that I
undertake to teach people and charge a fee for it, that is not true either.
e   Yet I think it a fine thing to be able to teach people as Gorgias of Leon-
tini does, and Prodicus of Ceos, and Hippias of Elis.⁴ Each of these
men can go to any city and persuade the young, who can keep company with anyone of their own fellow-citizens they want without
20   paying, to leave the company of these, to join with themselves, pay
them a fee, and be grateful to them besides. Indeed, I learned that
there is another wise man from Paros who is visiting us, for I met a
man who has spent more money on Sophists than everybody else put
together, Callias, the son of Hipponicus. So I asked him — he has two
sons — "Callias," I said, "if your sons were colts or calves, we could find
and engage a supervisor for them who would make them excel in their
b   proper qualities, some horse breeder or farmer. Now since they are
men, whom do you have in mind to supervise them? Who is an expert
in this kind of excellence, the human and social kind? I think you must
have given thought to this since you have sons. Is there such a person,"
I asked, "or is there not?" "Certainly there is," he said. "Who is he?" I
asked, "What is his name, where is he from? and what is his fee?" "His
name, Socrates, is Evenus, he comes from Paros, and his fee is five
c   minas." I thought Evenus a happy man, if he really possesses this art,
and teaches for so moderate a fee. Certainly I would pride and preen
myself if I had this knowledge, but I do not have it, gentlemen.

One of you might perhaps interrupt me and say: "But Socrates,
what is your occupation? From where have these slanders come? For
surely if you did not busy yourself with something out of the common,
all these rumours and talk would not have arisen unless you did something other than most people. Tell us what it is, that we may not speak
d   inadvisedly about you." Anyone who says that seems to be right, and I
will try to show you what has caused this reputation and slander.
Listen then. Perhaps some of you will think I am jesting, but be sure
that all that I shall say is true. What has caused my reputation is none
other than a certain kind of wisdom. What kind of wisdom? Human
wisdom, perhaps. It may be that I really possess this, while those whom

---

4. These were all well-known Sophists. Gorgias, after whom Plato named one of
his dialogues, was a celebrated rhetorician and teacher of rhetoric. He came to Athens
in 427 B.C., and his rhetorical tricks took the city by storm. Two dialogues, the
authenticity of which has been doubted, are named after Hippias, whose knowledge
was encyclopedic. Prodicus was known for his insistence on the precise meaning of
words. Both he and Hippias are characters in the *Protagoras* (named after another
famous Sophist).

I mentioned just now are wise with a wisdom more than human; else I   e
cannot explain it, for I certainly do not possess it, and whoever says I
do is lying and speaks to slander me. Do not create a disturbance,
gentlemen, even if you think I am boasting, for the story I shall tell
does not originate with me, but I will refer you to a trustworthy source.
I shall call upon the god at Delphi as witness to the existence and
nature of my wisdom, if it be such. You know Chairephon. He was my   21
friend from youth, and the friend of most of you, as he shared your exile and your return. You surely know the kind of man he was, how im-
pulsive in any course of action. He went to Delphi at one time and ventured to ask the oracle — as I say, gentlemen, do not create a disturbance — he asked if any man was wiser than I, and the Pythian re-
plied that no one was wiser. Chairephon is dead, but his brother will
testify to you about this.

Consider that I tell you this because I would inform you about the   b
origin of the slander. When I heard of this reply I asked myself: "Whatever does the god mean? What is his riddle? I am very conscious that I
am not wise at all; what then does he mean by saying that I am the
wisest? For surely he does not lie; it is not legitimate for him to do so."
For a long time I was at a loss as to his meaning; then I very reluctantly
turned to some such investigation as this: I went to one of those reputed
wise, thinking that there, if anywhere, I could refute the oracle and say   c
to it: "This man is wiser than I, but you said I was." Then, when I
examined this man — there is no need for me to tell you his name, he
was one of our public men — my experience was something like this: I
thought that he appeared wise to many people and especially to himself, but he was not. I then tried to show him that he thought himself
wise, but that he was not. As a result he came to dislike me, and so did   d
many of the bystanders. So I withdrew and thought to myself: "I am
wiser than this man; it is likely that neither of us knows anything
worthwhile, but he thinks he knows something when he does not,
whereas when I do not know, neither do I think I know; so I am likely
to be wiser than he to this small extent, that I do not think I know what
I do not know." After this I approached another man, one of those
thought to be wiser than he, and I thought the same thing, and so I   e
came to be disliked both by him and by many others.

After that I proceeded systematically. I realized, to my sorrow and
alarm, that I was getting unpopular, but I thought that I must attach
the greatest importance to the god's oracle, so I must go to all those who
had any reputation for knowledge to examine its meaning. And by the
dog,[5] gentlemen of the jury — for I must tell you the truth — I exper-   22

---

5. A curious oath, occasionally used by Socrates, it appears in a longer form in the
Gorgias (482b) as "by the dog, the god of the Egyptians."

ienced something like this: in my investigation in the service of the god
I found that those who had the highest reputation were nearly the most
deficient, while those who were thought to be inferior were more
knowledgeable. I must give you an account of my journeyings as if they
were labours I had undertaken to prove the oracle irrefutable. After the
politicians, I went to the poets, the writers of tragedies and dithyrambs

b   and the others, intending in their case to catch myself being more ignorant then they. So I took up those poems with which they seemed to
have taken most trouble and asked them what they meant, in order that
I might at the same time learn something from them. I am ashamed to
tell you the truth, gentlemen, but I must. Almost all the bystanders
might have explained the poems better than their authors could. I soon

c   realized that poets do not compose their poems with knowledge, but by
some inborn talent and by inspiration, like seers and prophets who also
say many fine things without any understanding of what they say. The
poets seemed to me to have had a similar experience. At the same time
I saw that, because of their poetry, they thought themselves very wise
men in other respects, which they were not. So there again I withdrew,
thinking that I had the same advantage over them as I had over the
politicians.

Finally I went to the craftsmen, for I was conscious of knowing

d   practically nothing, and I knew that I would find that they had knowledge of many fine things. In this I was not mistaken; they knew things I
did not know, and to that extent they were wiser than I. But, gentlemen of the jury, the good craftsmen seemed to me to have the same
fault as the poets: each of them, because of his success at his craft,
thought himself very wise in other most important pursuits, and this

e   error of theirs overshadowed the wisdom they had, so that I asked myself, on behalf of the oracle, whether I should prefer to be as I am, with
neither their wisdom nor their ignorance, or to have both. The answer
I gave myself and the oracle was that it was to my advantage to be as I
am.

As a result of this investigation, gentlemen of the jury, I acquired

23   much unpopularity, of a kind that is hard to deal with and is a heavy
burden; many slanders came from these people and a reputation for
wisdom, for in each case the bystanders thought that I myself possessed
the wisdom that I proved that my interlocutor did not have. What is
probable, gentlemen, is that in fact the god is wise and that his oracular
response meant that human wisdom is worth little or nothing, and that

b   when he says this man, Socrates, he is using my name as an example,
as if he said: "This man among you, mortals, is wisest who, like Socrates, understands that his wisdom is worthless." So even now I continue
this investigation as the god bade me — and I go around seeking out

anyone, citizen or stranger, whom I think wise. Then if I do not think he is, I come to the assistance of the god and show him that he is not wise. Because of this occupation, I do not have the leisure to engage in public affairs to any extent, nor indeed to look after my own, but I live in great poverty because of my service to the god.

Furthermore, the young men who follow me around of their own free will, those who have most leisure, the sons of the very rich, take pleasure in hearing people questioned; they themselves often imitate me and try to question others. I think they find an abundance of men who believe they have some knowledge but know little or nothing. The result is that those whom they question are angry, not with themselves but with me. They say: "That man Socrates is a pestilential fellow who corrupts the young." If one asks them what he does and what he teaches to corrupt them, they are silent, as they do not know, but, so as not to appear at a loss, they mention those accusations that are available against all philosophers, about "things in the sky and things below the earth," about "not believing in the gods" and "making the worse the stronger argument;" they would not want to tell the truth, I'm sure, that they have been proved to lay claim to knowledge when they know nothing. These people are ambitious, violent and numerous; they are continually and convincingly talking about me; they have been filling your ears for a long time with vehement slanders against me. From them Meletus attacked me, and Anytus and Lycon, Meletus being vexed on behalf of the poets, Anytus on behalf of the craftsmen and the politicians, Lycon on behalf of the orators, so that, as I started out by saying, I should be surprised if I could rid you of so much slander in so short a time. That, gentlemen of the jury, is the truth for you. I have hidden or disguised nothing. I know well enough that this very conduct makes me unpopular, and this is proof that what I say is true, that such is the slander against me, and that such are its causes. If you look into this either now or later, this is what you will find.

Let this suffice as a defence against the charges of my earlier accusers. After this I shall try to defend myself against Meletus, that good and patriotic man, as he says he is, and my later accusers. As these are a different lot of accusers, let us again take up their sworn deposition. It goes something like this: Socrates is guilty of corrupting the young and of not believing in the gods in whom the city believes, but in other new divinities. Such is their charge. Let us examine it point by point.

He says that I am guilty of corrupting the young, but I say that Meletus is guilty of dealing frivolously with serious matters, of irresponsibly bringing people into court, and of professing to be seriously concerned with things about none of which he has ever cared, and I shall try to prove that this is so. Come here and tell me, Meletus.

d   Surely you consider it of the greatest importance that our young men
       be as good as possible?[6] — Indeed I do.

       Come then, tell the jury who improves them. You obviously know,
       in view of your concern. You say you have discovered the one who cor-
       rupts them, namely me, and you bring me here and accuse me to the
       jury. Come, inform the jury and tell them who it is. You see, Meletus,
       that you are silent and know not what to say. Does this not seem
       shameful to you and a sufficient proof of what I say, that you have not
       been concerned with any of this? Tell me, my good sir, who improves
e   our young men? — The laws.

       That is not what I am asking, but what person who has knowledge
       of the laws to begin with? — These jurymen, Socrates.

       How do you mean, Meletus? Are these able to educate the young
       and improve them? — Certainly.

       All of them, or some but not others? — All of them.

       Very good, by Hera. You mention a great abundance of benefac-
25   tors. But what about the audience? Do they improve the young or not?
       — They do, too.

       What about the members of Council? — The Councillors, also.

       But, Meletus, what about the assembly? Do members of the assem-
       bly corrupt the young, or do they all improve them? — They improve
       them.

       All the Athenians, it seems, make the young into fine good men, ex-
       cept me, and I alone corrupt them. Is that what you mean? — That is
       most definitely what I mean.

b   You condemn me to a great misfortune. Tell me: does this also ap-
       ply to horses do you think? That all men improve them and one indi-
       vidual corrupts them? Or is quite the contrary true, one individual is
       able to improve them, or very few, namely the horse breeders, whereas
       the majority, if they have horses and use them, corrupt them? Is that
       not the case, Meletus, both with horses and all other animals? Of
       course it is, whether you and Anytus say so or not. It would be a very
       happy state of affairs if only one person corrupted our youth, while the
       others improved them.

c   You have made it sufficiently obvious, Meletus, that you have
       never had any concern for our youth; you show your indifference
       clearly; that you have given no thought to the subjects about which you
       bring me to trial.

       And by Zeus, Meletus, tell us also whether it is better for a man to
       live among good or wicked fellow-citizens. Answer, my good man, for I
       am not asking a difficult question. Do not the wicked do some harm to

---

6. Socrates here drops into his usual method of discussion by question and answer.
This, no doubt, is what Plato had in mind, at least in part, when he made him ask the
indulgence of the jury if he spoke "in his usual manner."

those who are ever closest to them, whereas good people benefit them? — Certainly.

And does the man exist who would rather be harmed than benefited   d
by his associates? Answer, my good sir, for the law orders you to answer. Is there any man who wants to be harmed? — Of course not.

Come now, do you accuse me here of corrupting the young and making them worse deliberately or unwillingly? — Deliberately.

What follows, Meletus? Are you so much wiser at your age than I am at mine that you understand that wicked people always do some harm to their closest neighbours while good people do them good, but I   e
have reached such a pitch of ignorance that I do not realize this, namely that if I make one of my associates wicked I run the risk of being harmed by him so that I do such a great evil deliberately, as you say? I do not believe you, Meletus, and I do not think anyone else will. Either I do not corrupt the young or, if I do, it is unwillingly, and you   26
are lying in either case. Now if I corrupt them unwillingly, the law does not require you to bring people to court for such unwilling wrong-doings, but to get hold of them privately, to instruct them and exhort them; for clearly, if I learn better, I shall cease to do what I am doing unwillingly. You, however, have avoided my company and were unwilling to instruct me, but you bring me here, where the law requires one to bring those who are in need of punishment, not of instruction.

And so, gentlemen of the jury, what I said is clearly true: Meletus has never been at all concerned with these matters. Nonetheless tell us,   b
Meletus, how you say that I corrupt the young; or is it obvious from your deposition that it is by teaching them not to believe in the gods in whom the city believes but in other new divinities? Is this not what you say I teach and so corrupt them? — That is most certainly what I do say.

Then by those very gods about whom we are talking, Meletus, make this clearer to me and to the jury: I cannot be sure whether you   c
mean that I teach the belief that there are some gods — and therefore I myself believe that there are gods and am not altogether an atheist, nor am I guilty of that — not, however, the gods in whom the city believes, but others, and that this is the charge against me, that they are others. Or whether you mean that I do not believe in gods at all, and that this is what I teach to others. — This is what I mean, that you do not believe in gods at all.

You are a strange fellow, Meletus. Why do you say this? Do I not   d
believe, as other men do, that the sun and the moon are gods? — No, by Zeus, jurymen, for he says that the sun is stone, and the moon earth.

My dear Meletus, do you think you are prosecuting Anaxagoras? Are you so contemptuous of the jury and think them so ignorant of letters as not to know that the books of Anaxagoras[7] of Clazomenae are full of those theories, and further, that the young men learn from me what they can buy from time to time for a drachma, at most, in the bookshops, and ridicule Socrates if he pretends that these theories are his own, especially as they are so absurd? Is that, by Zeus, what you think of me, Meletus, that I do not believe that there are any gods? — That is what I say, that you do not believe in the gods at all.

You cannot be believed, Meletus, even, I think, by yourself. The man appears to me, gentlemen of the jury, highly insolent and uncontrolled. He seems to have made this deposition out of insolence, violence and youthful zeal. He is like one who composed a riddle and is trying it out: "Will the wise Socrates realize that I am jesting and contradicting myself, or shall I deceive him and others?" I think he contradicts himself in the affidavit, as if he said: "Socrates is guilty of not believing in gods but believing in gods," and surely that is the part of a jester!

Examine with me, gentlemen, how he appears to contradict himself, and you, Meletus, answer us. Remember, gentlemen, what I asked you when I began, not to create a disturbance if I proceed in my usual manner.

Does any man, Meletus, believe in human affairs who does not believe in human beings? Make him answer, and not again and again create a disturbance. Does any man who does not believe in horses believe in equine affairs? Or in flute music but not in flute-players? No, my good sir, no man could. If you are not willing to answer, I will tell you and the jury. Answer the next question, however. Does any man believe in divine activities who does not believe in divinities? — No one.

Thank you for answering, if reluctantly, when the jury made you. Now you say that I believe in divine activities and teach about them, whether new or old, but at any rate divine activities according to what you say, and to this you have sworn in your deposition. But if I believe in divine activities I must quite inevitably believe in divine beings. Is that not so? It is indeed. I shall assume that you agree, as you do not answer. Do we not believe divine beings to be either gods or the children of gods? Yes or no? — Of course.

Then since I do believe in divine beings, as you admit, if divine beings are gods, this is what I mean when I say you speak in riddles and in jest, as you state that I do not believe in gods and then again that I

---

7. Anaxagoras of Clazomenae, born about the beginning of the fifth century B.C., came to Athens as a young man and spent his time in the pursuit of natural philosophy. He claimed that the universe was directed by Nous (Mind), and that matter was indestructible but always combining in various ways. He left Athens after being prosecuted for impiety.

do, since I believe in divine beings. If on the other hand the divine
beings are children of the gods, bastard children of the gods by nymphs
or some other mothers, as they are said to be, what man would believe
children of the gods to exist, but not gods? That would be just as absurd as to believe the young of horses and asses, namely mules, to exist,   e
but not to believe in the existence of horses and asses. You must have
made this deposition, Meletus, either to test us or because you were at
a loss to find any true wrongdoing of which to accuse me. There is no
way in which you could persuade anyone of even small intelligence that
it is not the part of one and the same man to believe in the activities of
divine beings and gods, and then again the part of one and the same   28
man not to believe in the existence of divinities and gods and heroes.

I do not think, gentlemen of the jury, that it requires a prolonged
defence to prove that I am not guilty of the charges in Meletus' deposition, but this is sufficient. On the other hand, you know that what I
said earlier is true, that I am very unpopular with many people. This
will be my undoing, if I am undone, not Meletus or Anytus but the
slanders and envy of many people. This has destroyed many other
good men and will, I think, continue to do so. There is no danger that   b
it will stop at me.

Someone might say: "Are you not ashamed, Socrates, to have followed the kind of occupation that has led to your being now in danger
of death?" However, I should be right to reply to him: "You are wrong,
sir, if you think that a man who is any good at all should take into account the risk of life or death; he should look to this only in his actions,
whether what he does is right or wrong, whether he is acting like a good
or a bad man." According to your view, all the heroes who died at Troy   c
were inferior people, especially the son of Thetis who was so contemptuous of danger compared with disgrace.[8] When he was eager to kill
Hector, his goddess mother warned him, as I believe, in some such
words as these: "My child, if you avenge the death of your comrade,
Patroclus, and you kill Hector, you will die yourself, for your death is
to follow immediately after Hector's." Hearing this, he despised death
and danger and was much more afraid to live a coward who did not
avenge his friends. "Let me die at once," he said, "when once I have   d
given the wrongdoer his deserts, rather than remain here, a laughingstock by the curved ships, a burden upon the earth." Do you think he
gave thought to death and danger?

This is the truth of the matter, gentlemen of the jury: wherever a
man has taken a position that he believes to be best, or has been placed
by his commander, there he must I think remain and face danger,
without a thought for death or anything else, rather than disgrace. It

---

8. The scene between Thetis and Achilles is from the *Iliad* (18, 94ff.).

e   would have been a dreadful way to behave, gentlemen of the jury, if, at Potidaea, Amphipolis and Delium, I had, at the risk of death, like anyone else, remained at my post where those you had elected to command had ordered me, and then, when the god ordered me, as I thought and believed, to live the life of a philosopher, to examine myself and others,

29   I had abandoned my post for fear of death or anything else. That would have been a dreadful thing, and then I might truly have justly been brought here for not believing that there are gods, disobeying the oracle, fearing death, and thinking I was wise when I was not. To fear death, gentlemen, is no other than to think oneself wise when one is not, to think one knows what one does not know. No one knows whether death may not be the greatest of all blessings for a man, yet men fear it as if they knew that it is the greatest of evils. And surely it is

b   the most blameworthy ignorance to believe that one knows what one does not know. It is perhaps on this point and in this respect, gentlemen, that I differ from the majority of men, and if I were to claim that I am wiser than anyone in anything, it would be in this, that, as I have no adequate knowledge of things in the underworld, so I do not think I have. I do know, however, that it is wicked and shameful to do wrong, to disobey one's superior, be he god or man. I shall never fear or avoid things of which I do not know, whether they may not be good rather

c   than things that I know to be bad. Even if you acquitted me now and did not believe Anytus, who said to you that either I should not have been brought here in the first place, or that now I am here, you cannot avoid executing me, for if I should be acquitted, your sons would practise the teachings of Socrates and all be thoroughly corrupted; if you said to me in this regard: "Socrates, we do not believe Anytus now; we acquit you, but only on condition that you spend no more time on this investigation and do not practise philosophy, and if you are caught

d   doing so you will die;" if, as I say, you were to acquit me on those terms, I would say to you: "Gentlemen of the jury, I am grateful and I am your friend, but I will obey the god rather than you, and as long as I draw breath and am able, I shall not cease to practise philosophy, to exhort you and in my usual way to point out to any one of you whom I happen to meet: Good Sir, you are an Athenian, a citizen of the greatest city with the greatest reputation for both wisdom and power;

e   are you not ashamed of your eagerness to possess as much wealth, reputation and honours as possible, while you do not care for nor give thought to wisdom or truth, or the best possible state of your soul?" Then, if one of you disputes this and says he does care, I shall not let him go at once or leave him, but I shall question him, examine him and test him, and if I do not think he has attained the goodness that he says he has, I shall reproach him because he attaches little

30   importance to the most important things and greater importance to

inferior things. I shall treat in this way anyone I happen to meet, young
and old, citizen and stranger, and more so the citizens because you are
more kindred to me. Be sure that this is what the god orders me to do,
and I think there is no greater blessing for the city than my service to
the god. For I go around doing nothing but persuading both young and
old among you not to care for your body or your wealth in preference to   b
or as strongly as for the best possible state of your soul, as I say to you:
"Wealth does not bring about excellence, but excellence brings about
wealth and all other public and private blessings for men."

Now if by saying this I corrupt the young, this advice must be
harmful, but if anyone says that I give different advice, he is talking
nonsense. On this point I would say to you, gentlemen of the jury:
"Whether you believe Anytus or not, whether you acquit me or not, do
so on the understanding that this is my course of action, even if I am to   c
face death many times." Do not create a disturbance, gentlemen, but
abide by my request not to cry out at what I say but to listen, for I think
it will be to your advantage to listen, and I am about to say other things
at which you will perhaps cry out. By no means do this. Be sure that if
you kill the sort of man I say I am, you will not harm me more than
yourselves. Neither Meletus nor Anytus can harm me in any way; he
could not harm me, for I do not think it is permitted that a better man   d
be harmed by a worse; certainly he might kill me, or perhaps banish or
disfranchise me, which he and maybe others think to be great harm,
but I do not think so. I think he is doing himself much greater harm doing what he is doing now, attempting to have a man executed unjustly.
Indeed, gentlemen of the jury, I am far from making a defence now on
my own behalf, as might be thought, but on yours, to prevent you from
wrongdoing by mistreating the god's gift to you by condemning me; for   e
if you kill me you will not easily find another like me. I was attached to
this city by the god — though it seems a ridiculous thing to say — as
upon a great and noble horse which was somewhat sluggish because of
its size and needed to be stirred up by a kind of gadfly. It is to fulfill
some such function that I believe the god has placed me in the city. I
never cease to rouse each and every one of you, to persuade and reproach you all day long and everywhere I find myself in your company.   31

Another such man will not easily come to be among you, gentlemen, and if you believe me you will spare me. You might easily be
annoyed with me as people are when they are aroused from a doze, and
strike out at me; if convinced by Anytus you could easily kill me, and
then you could sleep on for the rest of your days, unless the god, in his
care for you, sent you someone else. That I am the kind of person to be
a gift of the god to the city you might realize from the fact that it does
not seem like human nature for me to have neglected all my own affairs   b
and to have tolerated this neglect now for so many years while I was al-

ways concerned with you, approaching each one of you like a father or an elder brother to persuade you to care for virtue. Now if I profited from this by charging a fee for my advice, there would be some sense to it, but you can see for yourselves that, for all their shameless accusations, my accusers have not been able in their impudence to bring for-
c ward a witness to say that I have ever received a fee or ever asked for one. I, on the other hand, have a convincing witness that I speak the truth, my poverty.

It may seem strange that while I go around and give this advice privately and interfere in private affairs, I do not venture to go to the assembly and there advise the city. You have heard me give the reason for this in many places. I have a divine sign from the god which Mele-
d tus has ridiculed in his deposition. This began when I was a child. It is a voice, and whenever it speaks it turns me away from something I am about to do, but it never encourages me to do anything. This is what has prevented me from taking part in public affairs, and I think it was quite right to prevent me. Be sure, gentlemen of the jury, that if I had long ago attempted to take part in politics, I should have died long ago,
e and benefited neither you nor myself. Do not be angry with me for speaking the truth; no man will survive who genuinely opposes you or any other crowd and prevents the occurrence of many unjust and il-
32 legal happenings in the city. A man who really fights for justice must lead a private, not a public, life if he is to survive for even a short time.

I shall give you great proofs of this, not words but what you esteem, deeds. Listen to what happened to me, that you may know that I will not yield to any man contrary to what is right, for fear of death, even if I should die at once for not yielding. The things I shall tell you are commonplace and smack of the lawcourts, but they are true. I have never
b held any other office in the city, but I served as a member of the Council, and our tribe Antiochis was presiding at the time when you wanted to try as a body the ten generals who had failed to pick up the survivors of the naval battle.[9] This was illegal, as you all recognized later. I was the only member of the presiding committee to oppose your doing something contrary to the laws, and I voted against it. The orators were ready to prosecute me and take me away, and your shouts were egging them on, but I thought I should run any risk on the side of law

9. This was the battle of Arginusae (south of Lesbos) in 406 B.C., the last Athenian victory of the war. A violent storm prevented the Athenian generals from rescuing their survivors. For this they were tried in Athens and sentenced to death by the assembly. They were tried in a body, and it is this to which Socrates objected in the Council's presiding committee which prepared the business of the assembly. He obstinately persisted in his opposition, in which he stood alone, and was overruled by the majority. Six generals who were in Athens were executed.

and justice rather than join you, for fear of prison or death, when you   c
were engaged in an unjust course.

This happened when the city was still a democracy. When the oligarchy was established, the Thirty[10] summoned me to the Hall, along
with four others, and ordered us to bring Leon from Salamis, that he
might be executed. They gave many such orders to many people, in
order to implicate as many as possible in their guilt. Then I showed   d
again, not in words but in action, that, if it were not rather vulgar to
say so, death is something I couldn't care less about, but that my whole
concern is not to do anything unjust or impious. That government,
powerful as it was, did not frighten me into any wrongdoing. When we
left the Hall, the other four went to Salamis and brought in Leon, but I
went home. I might have been put to death for this, had not the
government fallen shortly afterwards. There are many who will witness   e
to these events.

Do you think I would have survived all these years if I were
engaged in public affairs and, acting as a good man must, came to the
help of justice and considered this the most important thing? Far from
it, gentlemen of the jury, nor would any other man. Throughout my
life, in any public activity I may have engaged in, I am the same man   33
as I am in private life. I have never come to an agreement with anyone
to act unjustly, neither with anyone else nor with any one of those who
they slanderously say are my pupils. I have never been anyone's
teacher. If anyone, young or old, desires to listen to me when I am talking and dealing with my own concerns, I have never begrudged this to
anyone, but I do not converse when I receive a fee and not when I do
not. I am equally ready to question the rich and the poor if anyone is   b
willing to answer my questions and listen to what I say. And I cannot
justly be held responsible for the good or bad conduct of these people,
as I never promised to teach them anything and have not done so. If
anyone says that he has learned anything from me, or that he heard
anything privately that the others did not hear, be assured that he is not
telling the truth.

Why then do some people enjoy spending considerable time in my
company? You have heard why, gentlemen of the jury, I have told you   c
the whole truth. They enjoy hearing those being questioned who think
they are wise, but are not. And this is not unpleasant. To do this has,
as I say, been enjoined upon me by the god, by means of oracles and
dreams, and in every other way that a divine manifestation has ever

---

10. This was the harsh oligarchy that was set up after the final defeat of Athens in
404 B.C. and that ruled Athens for some nine months in 404-3 before the democracy was
restored.

ordered a man to do anything. This is true, gentlemen, and can easily be established.

d   If I corrupt some young men and have corrupted others, then surely some of them who have grown older and realized that I gave them bad advice when they were young should now themselves come up here to accuse me and avenge themselves. If they were unwilling to do so themselves, then some of their kindred, their fathers or brothers or other relations should recall it now if their family had been harmed by me. I see many of these present here, first Crito, my contemporary e   and fellow demesman, the father of Critoboulos here; next Lysanias of Sphettus, the father of Aeschines here; also Antiphon the Cephisian, the father of Epigenes; and others whose brothers spent their time in this way; Nicostratus, the son of Theozotides, brother of Theodotus, and Theodotus has died so he could not influence him; Paralios here, 34   son of Demodocus, whose brother was Theages; there is Adeimantus, son of Ariston, brother of Plato here; Acantidorus, brother of Apollodorus here.

I could mention many others, some one of whom surely Meletus should have brought in as witness in his own speech. If he forgot to do so, then let him do it now; I will yield time if he has anything of the kind to say. You will find quite the contrary, gentlemen. These men are all ready to come to the help of the corruptor, the man who has b   harmed their kindred, as Meletus and Anytus say. Now those who were corrupted might well have reason to help me, but the uncorrupted, their kindred who are older men, have no reason to help me except the right and proper one, that they know that Meletus is lying and that I am telling the truth.

Very well, gentlemen of the jury. This, and maybe other similar things, is what I have to say in my defence. Perhaps one of you might c   be angry as he recalls that when he himself stood trial on a less dangerous charge, he begged and implored the jury with many tears, that he brought his children and many of his friends and family into court to arouse as much pity as he could, but that I do none of these things, even though I may seem to be running the ultimate risk. Thinking of d   this, he might feel resentful toward me and, angry about this, cast his vote in anger. If there is such a one among you — I do not deem there is, but if there is — I think it would be right to say in reply: My good sir, I too have a household and, in Homer's phrase, I am not born "from oak or rock" but from men, so that I have a family, indeed three sons, gentlemen of the jury, of whom one is an adolescent while two are children. Nevertheless, I will not beg you to acquit me by bringing them here. Why do I do none of these things? Not through arrogance, e   gentlemen, nor through lack of respect for you. Whether I am brave in the face of death is another matter, but with regard to my reputation and yours and that of the whole city, it does not seem right to me to do these things, especially at my age and with my reputation. For it is generally believed, whether it be true or false, that in certain respects Socrates is superior to the majority of men. Now if those of you who are 35 considered superior, be it in wisdom or courage or whatever other virtue makes them so, are seen behaving like that, it would be a disgrace. Yet I have often seen them do this sort of thing when standing trial, men who are thought to be somebody, doing amazing things as if they thought it a terrible thing to die, and as if they were to be immortal if you did not execute them. I think these men bring shame upon the city so that a stranger, too, would assume that those who are outstanding in b virtue among the Athenians, whom they themselves select from themselves to fill offices of state and receive other honours, are in no way better than women. You should not act like that, gentlemen of the jury, those of you who have any reputation at all, and if we do, you should not allow it. You should make it very clear that you will more readily convict a man who performs these pitiful dramatics in court and so makes the city a laughingstock, than a man who keeps quiet.

Quite apart from the question of reputation, gentlemen, I do not think it right to supplicate the jury and to be acquitted because of this, c but to teach and persuade them. It is not the purpose of a juryman's office to give justice as a favour to whoever seems good to him, but to judge according to law, and this he has sworn to do. We should not accustom you to perjure yourselves, nor should you make a habit of it. This is irreverent conduct for either of us.

Do not deem it right for me, gentlemen of the jury, that I should act towards you in a way that I do not consider to be good or just or pious, d especially, by Zeus, as I am being prosecuted by Meletus here for impiety; clearly, if I convinced you by my supplication to do violence to your oath of office, I would be teaching you not to believe that there are gods, and my defence would convict me of not believing in them. This is far from being the case, gentlemen, for I do believe in them as none of my accusers do. I leave it to you and the god to judge me in the way that will be best for me and for you.

[The jury now gives its verdict of guilty, and Meletus asks for the penalty of death.]

There are many other reasons for my not being angry with you for e convicting me, gentlemen of the jury, and what happened was not unexpected. I am much more surprised at the number of votes cast on 36 each side, for I did not think the decision would be by so few votes but by a great many. As it is, a switch of only thirty votes would have acquitted me. I think myself that I have been cleared on Meletus'

b   charges, and not only this, but it is clear to all that, if Anytus and Lycon had not joined him in accusing me, he would have been fined a
thousand drachmas for not receiving a fifth of the votes.

He assesses the penalty at death. So be it. What counter-assessment
should I propose to you, gentlemen of the jury? Clearly it should be a
penalty I deserve, and what do I deserve to suffer or to pay because I
have deliberately not led a quiet life but have neglected what occupies
most people: wealth, household affairs, the position of general or public
orator or the other offices, the political clubs and factions that exist in
the city? I thought myself too honest to survive if I occupied myself
c   with those things. I did not follow that path that would have made me
of no use either to you or to myself, but I went to each of you privately
and conferred upon him what I say is the greatest benefit, by trying to
persuade him not to care for any of his belongings before caring that he
himself should be as good and as wise as possible, not to care for the
city's possessions more than for the city itself, and to care for other
d   things in the same way. What do I deserve for being such a man? Some
good, gentlemen of the jury, if I must truly make an assessment according to my deserts, and something suitable. What is suitable for a poor
benefactor who needs leisure to exhort you? Nothing is more suitable,
gentlemen, than for such a man to be fed in the Prytaneum,[11] much
more suitable for him than for any one of you who has won a victory at
Olympia with a pair or a team of horses. The Olympian victor makes
e   you think yourself happy; I make you be happy. Besides, he does not
need food, but I do. So if I must make a just assessment of what I de-
37   serve, I assess it at this: free meals in the Prytaneum.

When I say this you may think, as when I spoke of appeals to pity
and entreaties, that I speak arrogantly, but that is not the case, gentlemen of the jury; rather it is like this: I am convinced that I never willingly wrong anyone, but I am not convincing you of this, for we have
talked together but a short time. If it were the law with us, as it is else-
b   where, that a trial for life should not last one but many days, you would
be convinced, but now it is not easy to dispel great slanders in a short
time. Since I am convinced that I wrong no one, I am not likely to
wrong myself, to say that I deserve some evil and to make some such
assessment against myself. What should I fear? That I should suffer the
penalty Meletus has assessed against me, of which I say I do not know
whether it is good or bad? Am I then to choose in preference to this
something that I know very well to be an evil and assess the penalty at
c   that? Imprisonment? Why should I live in prison, always subjected to
the ruling magistrates the Eleven? A fine, and imprisonment until I

---

11. The Prytaneum was the magistrates' hall or town hall of Athens in which public
entertainments were given, particularly to Olympian victors on their return home.

pay it? That would be the same thing for me, as I have no money. Exile? for perhaps you might accept that assessment.

I should have to be inordinately fond of life, gentlemen of the jury, to be so unreasonable as to suppose that other men will easily tolerate my company and conversation when you, my fellow citizens, have been unable to endure them, but found them a burden and resented   d
them so that you are now seeking to get rid of them. Far from it, gentlemen. It would be a fine life at my age to be driven out of one city after another, for I know very well that wherever I go the young men will listen to my talk as they do here. If I drive them away, they will them-   e
selves persuade their elders to drive me out; if I do not drive them away, their fathers and relations will drive me out on their behalf.

Perhaps someone might say: But Socrates, if you leave us will you not be able to live quietly, without talking? Now this is the most difficult point on which to convince some of you. If I say that it is impossible for me to keep quiet because that means disobeying the god, you   38
will not believe me and will think I am being ironical. On the other hand, if I say that it is the greatest good for a man to discuss virtue every day and those other things about which you hear me conversing and testing myself and others, for the unexamined life is not worth living for man, you will believe me even less.

What I say is true, gentlemen, but it is not easy to convince you. At the same time, I am not accustomed to think that I deserve any penal-   b
ty. If I had money, I would assess the penalty at the amount I could pay, for that would not hurt me, but I have none, unless you are willing to set the penalty at the amount I can pay, and perhaps I could pay you one mina of silver.[12] So that is my assessment.

Plato here, gentlemen of the jury, and Crito and Critoboulus and Apollodorus bid me put the penalty at thirty minae, and they will stand surety for the money. Well then, that is my assessment, and they will be sufficient guarantee of payment.

[The jury now votes again and sentences Socrates to death.]

It is for the sake of a short time, gentlemen of the jury, that you will   c
acquire the reputation and the guilt, in the eyes of those who want to denigrate the city, of having killed Socrates, a wise man, for they who want to revile you will say that I am wise even if I am not. If you had waited but a little while, this would have happened of its own accord. You see my age, that I am already advanced in years and close to death. I am saying this not to all of you but to those who condemned   d

---

12. One mina was 100 drachmas, equivalent to, say, twenty-five dollars, though in purchasing power probably five times greater. In any case, a ridiculously small sum under the circumstances.

me to death, and to these same jurors I say: Perhaps you think that I was convicted for lack of such words as might have convinced you, if I thought I should say or do all I could to avoid my sentence. Far from it. I was convicted because I lacked not words but boldness and shamelessness and the willingness to say to you what you would most gladly have heard from me, lamentations and tears and my saying and doing

e   many things that I say are unworthy of me but that you are accustomed to hear from others. I did not think then that the danger I ran should make me do anything mean, nor do I now regret the nature of my defence. I would much rather die after this kind of defence than live after making the other kind. Neither I nor any other man should, on trial or

39   in war, contrive to avoid death at any cost. Indeed it is often obvious in battle that one could escape death by throwing away one's weapons and by turning to supplicate one's pursuers, and there are many ways to avoid death in every kind of danger if one will venture to do or say anything to avoid it. It is not difficult to avoid death, gentlemen of the jury,

b   it is much more difficult to avoid wickedness, for it runs faster than death. Slow and elderly as I am, I have been caught by the slower pursuer, whereas my accusers, being clever and sharp, have been caught by the quicker, wickedness. I leave you now, condemned to death by you, but they are condemned by truth to wickedness and injustice. So I maintain my assessment, and they maintain theirs. This perhaps had to happen, and I think it is as it should be.

c   Now I want to prophesy to those who convicted me, for I am at the point when men prophesy most, when they are about to die. I say gentlemen, to those who voted to kill me, that vengeance will come upon you immediately after my death, a vengeance much harder to bear than that which you took in killing me. You did this in the belief that you would avoid giving an account of your life, but I maintain that quite the opposite will happen to you. There will be more people to test

d   you, whom I now held back, but you did not notice it. They will be more difficult to deal with as they will be younger and you will resent them more. You are wrong if you believe that by killing people you will prevent anyone from reproaching you for not living in the right way. To escape such tests is neither possible nor good, but it is best and easiest not to discredit others but to prepare oneself to be as good as possible. With this prophecy to you who convicted me, I part from you.

e   I should be glad to discuss what has happened with those who voted for my acquittal during the time that the officers of the court are busy and I do not yet have to depart to my death. So, gentlemen, stay with me awhile, for nothing prevents us from talking to each other while it is

40   allowed. To you, as being my friends, I want to show the meaning of what has occurred. A surprising thing has happened to me, judges — you I would rightly call judges. At all previous times my usual mantic

sign frequently opposed me, even in small matters, when I was about
to do something wrong, but now that, as you can see for yourselves, I
was faced with what one might think, and what is generally thought to
be, the worst of evils, my divine sign has not opposed me, either when I
left home at dawn, or when I came into court, or at any time that I was
about to say something during my speech. Yet in other talks it often
held me back in the middle of my speaking, but now it has opposed no
word or deed of mine. What do I think is the reason for this? I will tell
you. What has happened to me may well be a good thing, and those of
us who believe death to be an evil are certainly mistaken. I have convincing proof of this, for it is impossible that my customary sign did not
oppose me if I was not about to do what was right.

    Let us reflect in this way, too, that there is good hope that death is a
blessing, for it is one of two things: either the dead are nothing and
have no perception of anything, or it is, as we are told, a change and a
relocating for the soul from here to another place. If it is complete lack
of perception, like a dreamless sleep, then death would be a great advantage. For I think that if one had to pick out that night during which
a man slept soundly and did not dream, put beside it the other nights
and days of his life, and then see how many days and nights had been
better and more pleasant than that night, not only a private person but
the great king would find them easy to count compared with the other
days and nights. If death is like this I say it is an advantage, for all eter-
nity would then seem to be no more than a single night. If, on the other
hand, death is a change from here to another place, and what we are
told is true and all who have died are there, what greater blessing could
there be, gentlemen of the jury? If anyone arriving in Hades will have
escaped from those who call themselves judges here, and will find those
true judges who are said to sit in judgement there, Minos and Rada-
manthus and Aeacus and Triptolemus and the other demi-gods who
have been upright in their own life, would that be a poor kind of
change? Again, what would one of you give to keep company with Or-
pheus and Musaeus, Hesiod and Homer? I am willing to die many
times if that is true. It would be a wonderful way for me to spend my
time whenever I met Palamedes and Ajax, the son of Telamon, and
any other of the men of old who died through an unjust conviction, to
compare my experience with theirs. I think it would be pleasant. Most
important, I could spend my time testing and examining people there,
as I do here, as to who among them is wise, and who thinks he is, but is
not.

    What would one not give, gentlemen of the jury, for the oppor-
tunity to examine the man who led the great expedition against Troy,
or Odysseus, or Sisyphus, and innumerable other men and women one
could mention. It would be an extraordinary happiness to talk with

them, to keep company with them and examine them. In any case, they would certainly not put one to death for doing so. They are happier there than we are here in other respects, and for the rest of time they are deathless, if indeed what we are told is true.

You too must be of good hope as regards death, gentlemen of the jury, and keep this one truth in mind, that a good man cannot be

d   harmed either in life or in death, and that his affairs are not neglected by the gods. What has happened to me now has not happened of itself, but it is clear to me that it was better for me to die now and to escape from trouble. That is why my divine sign did not oppose me at any point. So I am certainly not angry with those who convicted me, or with my accusers. Of course that was not their purpose when they accused and convicted me, but they thought they were hurting me, and

e   for this they deserve blame. This much I ask from them: when my sons grow up, avenge yourselves by causing them the same kind of grief that I caused you, if you think they care for money or anything else more than they care for virtue, or if they think they are somebody when they are nobody. Reproach them as I reproach you, that they do not care for the right things and think they are worthy when they are not worthy of

42   anything. If you do this, I shall have been justly treated by you, and my sons also.

Now the hour to part has come. I go to die, you go to live. Which of us goes to the better lot is known to no one, except the god.

CRITO

About the time of Socrates' trial, a state galley had set out on an annual religious mission to Delos and while it was away no execution was allowed to take place. So it was that Socrates was kept in prison for a month after the trial. The ship has now arrived at Cape Sunium in Attica and is thus expected at the Piraeus momentarily. So Socrates' old and faithful friend, Crito, makes one last effort to persuade him to escape into exile, and all arrangements for this plan have been made. It is this conversation between the two old friends that Plato professes to report in this dialogue. It is, as Crito plainly tells him, his last chance, but Socrates will not take it, and he gives his reasons for his refusal. Whether this conversation took place at this particular time is not important, for there is every reason to believe that Socrates' friends tried to plan his escape, and that he refused. Plato more than hints that the authorities would not have minded much, as long as he left the country.

SOCRATES: Why have you come so early, Crito? Or is it not still 43 early?

CRITO: It certainly is.

S: How early?

C: Early dawn.

S: I am surprised that the warder was willing to listen to you.

C: He is quite friendly to me by now, Socrates. I have been here often and I have given him something.

S: Have you just come, or have you been here for some time?

C: A fair time.

S: Then why did you not wake me right away but sit there in b silence?

C: By Zeus no, Socrates. I would not myself want to be in distress and awake so long. I have been surprised to see you so peacefully asleep. It was on purpose that I did not wake you, so that you should spend your time most agreeably. Often in the past throughout my life, I have considered the way you live happy, and especially so now that you bear your present misfortune so easily and lightly.

S: It would not be fitting at my age to resent the fact that I must die now.

c

C: Other men of your age are caught in such misfortunes, but their age does not prevent them resenting their fate.

S: That is so. Why have you come so early?

C: I bring bad news, Socrates, not for you, apparently, but for me and all your friends the news is bad and hard to bear. Indeed, I would count it among the hardest.

d

S: What is it? Or has the ship arrived from Delos, at the arrival of which I must die?

C: It has not arrived yet, but it will, I believe, arrive today, according to a message brought by some men from Sunium, where they left it. This makes it obvious that it will come today, and that your life must end tomorrow.

S: May it be for the best. If it so please the gods, so be it. However, I do not think it will arrive today.

44

C: What indication have you of this?

S: I will tell you. I must die the day after the ship arrives.

C: That is what those in authority say.

S: Then I do not think it will arrive on this coming day, but on the next. I take to witness of this a dream I had a little earlier during this night. It looks as if it was the right time for you not to wake me.

C: What was your dream?

S: I thought that a beautiful and comely woman dressed in white approached me. She called me and said: "Socrates, may you arrive at fertile Phthia[1] on the third day."

b

C: A strange dream, Socrates.

S: But it seems clear enough to me, Crito.

---

1. A quotation from the ninth book of the *Iliad* (363). Achilles has rejected all the presents of Agamemnon for him to return to the battle, and threatens to go home. He says his ships will sail in the morning, and with good weather he might arrive on the third day "in fertile Phthia" (which is his home). The dream means, obviously, that on the third day Socrates' soul, after death, will find its home. As always, counting the first member of a series, the third day is the day after tomorrow.

C: Too clear it seems, my dear Socrates, but listen to me even now and be saved. If you die, it will not be a single misfortune for me. Not only will I be deprived of a friend, the like of whom I shall never find again, but many people who do not know you or me very well will think that I could have saved you if I were willing to spend money, but that I did not care to do so. Surely there can be no worse reputation than to be thought to value money more highly than one's friends, for the majority will not believe that you yourself were not willing to leave prison while we were eager for you to do so.

c

S: My good Crito, why should we care so much for what the majority think? The most reasonable people, to whom one should pay more attention, will believe that things were done as they were done.

C: You see, Socrates, that one must also pay attention to the opinion of the majority. Your present situation makes clear that the majority can inflict not the least but pretty well the greatest evils if one is slandered among them.

d

S: Would that the majority could inflict the greatest evils, for they would then be capable of the greatest good, and that would be fine, but now they cannot do either. They cannot make a man either wise or foolish, but they inflict things haphazardly.

C: That may be so. But tell me this, Socrates, are you anticipating that I and your other friends would have trouble with the informers if you escape from here, as having stolen you away, and that we should be compelled to lose all our property or pay heavy fines and suffer other punishment besides? If you have any such fear, forget it. We would be justified in running this risk to save you, and worse, if necessary. Do follow my advice, and do not act differently.

e

45

S: I do have these things in mind, Crito, and also many others.

C: Have no such fear. It is not much money that some people require to save you and get you out of here. Further, do you not see that those informers are cheap, and that not much money would be needed to deal with them? My money is available and is, I think, sufficient. If, because of your affection for me, you feel you should not spend any of mine, there are those strangers here ready to spend money. One of them, Simmias the Theban, has brought enough for this very purpose. Cebes, too, and a good many others. So, as I say, do not let this fear make you hesitate to save yourself, nor let what you said in court trouble you, that you would not know what to do with yourself if you left Athens, for you would be welcomed in many places to which you might go. If you want to go to Thessaly, I have friends there who will greatly appreciate you and keep you safe, so that no one in Thessaly will harm you.

b

c

Besides, Socrates, I do not think that what you are doing is right, to give up your life when you can save it, and to hasten your fate as your enemies would hasten it, and indeed have hastened it in their wish to destroy you. Moreover, I think you are betraying your sons by going

d   away and leaving them, when you could bring them up and educate them. You thus show no concern for what their fate may be. They will probably have the usual fate of orphans. Either one should not have children, or one should share with them to the end the toil of upbringing and education. You seem to me to choose the easiest path, whereas one should choose the path a good and courageous man would choose, particularly when one claims throughout one's life to care for virtue.

e   I feel ashamed on your behalf and on behalf of us, your friends, lest all that has happened to you be thought due to cowardice on our part: the fact that your trial came to court when it need not have done so, the handling of the trial itself, and now this absurd ending which will be thought to have got beyond our control through some cowardice and

46   unmanliness on our part, since we did not save you, or you save yourself, when it was possible and could be done if we had been of the slightest use. Consider, Socrates, whether this is not only evil, but shameful, both for you and for us. Take counsel with yourself, or rather the time for counsel is past and the decision should have been taken, and there is no further opportunity, for this whole business must be ended tonight. If we delay now, then it will no longer be possible, it will be too late. Let me persuade you on every count, Socrates, and do not act otherwise.

b   S: My dear Crito, your eagerness is worth much if it should have some right aim; if not, then the greater your keenness the more difficult it is to deal with. We must therefore examine whether we should act in this way or not, as not only now but at all times I am the kind of man who listens only to the argument that on reflection seems best to me. I cannot, now that this fate has come upon me, discard the arguments I used; they seem to me much the same. I value and respect the same

c   principles as before, and if we have no better arguments to bring up at this moment, be sure that I shall not agree with you, not even if the power of the majority were to frighten us with more bogeys, as if we were children, with threats of incarcerations and executions and confiscation of property. How should we examine this matter most reasonably? Would it be by taking up first your argument about the opinions of men, whether it is sound in every case that one should pay attention

d   to some opinions, but not to others? Or was that well-spoken before the necessity to die came upon me, but now it is clear that this was said in vain for the sake of argument, that it was in truth play and nonsense?

I am eager to examine together with you, Crito, whether this argument will appear in any way different to me in my present circumstances, or whether it remains the same, whether we are to abandon it or believe it. It was said on every occasion by those who thought they were speaking sensibly, as I have just now been speaking, that one should greatly value some people's opinions, but not others. Does that seem to you a sound statement? e

You, as far as a human being can tell, are exempt from the likelihood of dying tomorrow, so the present misfortune is not likely to lead you astray. Consider then, do you not think it a sound statement that one must not value all the opinions of men, but some and not others, nor the opinions of all men, but those of some and not of others? What do you say? Is this not well said? 47

C: It is.

S: One should value the good opinions, and not the bad ones?

C: Yes.

S: The good opinions are those of wise men, the bad ones those of foolish men?

C: Of course.

S: Come then, what of statements such as this: Should a man professionally engaged in physical training pay attention to the praise and blame and opinion of any man, or to those of one man only, namely a doctor or trainer? b

C: To those of one only.

S: He should therefore fear the blame and welcome the praise of that one man, and not those of the many?

C: Obviously.

S: He must then act and exercise, eat and drink in the way the one, the trainer and the one who knows, thinks right, not all the others?

C: That is so.

S: Very well. And if he disobeys the one, disregards his opinion and his praises while valuing those of the many who have no knowledge, will he not suffer harm? c

C: Of course.

S: What is that harm, where does it tend, and what part of the man who disobeys does it affect?

C: Obviously the harm is to his body, which it ruins.

S: Well said. So with other matters, not to enumerate them all, and certainly with actions just and unjust, shameful and beautiful, good and bad, about which we are now deliberating, should we follow d the opinion of the many and fear it, or that of the one, if there is one who has knowledge of these things and before whom we feel fear and shame more than before all the others. If we do not follow his directions, we shall harm and corrupt that part of ourselves that is improved by just actions and destroyed by unjust actions. Or is there nothing in this?

C: I think there certainly is, Socrates.

S: Come now, if we ruin that which is improved by health and corrupted by disease by not following the opinions of those who know,
e is life worth living for us when that is ruined? And that is the body, is it not?

C: Yes.

S: And is life worth living with a body that is corrupted and in bad condition?

C: In no way.

S: And is life worth living for us with that part of us corrupted that unjust action harms and just action benefits? Or do we think that part of us, whatever it is, that is concerned with justice and injustice, is
48 inferior to the body?

C: Not at all.

S: It is more valuable?

C: Much more.

S: We should not then think so much of what the majority will say about us, but what he will say who understands justice and injustice, the one, that is, and the truth itself. So that, in the first place, you were wrong to believe that we should care for the opinion of the many about what is just, beautiful, good, and their opposites. "But," someone might say "the many are able to put us to death."

b C: That too is obvious, Socrates, and someone might well say so.

S: And, my admirable friend, that argument that we have gone through remains, I think, as before. Examine the following statement in turn as to whether it stays the same or not, that the most important thing is not life, but the good life.

C: It stays the same.

S: And that the good life, the beautiful life, and the just life are the same; does that still hold, or not?

C: It does hold.

S: As we have agreed so far, we must examine next whether it is
c right for me to try to get out of here when the Athenians have not acquitted me. If it is seen to be right, we will try to do so; if it is not, we

will abandon the idea. As for those questions you raise about money, reputation, the upbringing of children, Crito, those considerations in truth belong to those people who easily put men to death and would bring them to life again if they could, without thinking; I mean the majority of men. For us, however, since our argument leads to this, the only valid consideration, as we were saying just now, is whether we should be acting rightly in giving money and gratitude to those who will lead me out of here, and ourselves helping with the escape, or whether in truth we shall do wrong in doing all this. If it appears that we shall be acting unjustly, then we have no need at all to take into account whether we shall have to die if we stay here and keep quiet, or suffer in another way, rather than do wrong.

C: I think you put that beautifully, Socrates, but see what we should do.

S: Let us examine the question together, my dear friend, and if you can make any objection while I am speaking, make it and I will listen to you, but if you have no objection to make, my dear Crito, then stop now from saying the same thing so often, that I must leave here against the will of the Athenians. I think it important to persuade you before I act, and not to act against your wishes. See whether the start of our enquiry is adequately stated, and try to answer what I ask you in the way you think best.

C: I shall try.

S: Do we say that one must never in any way do wrong willingly, or must one do wrong in one way and not in another? Is to do wrong never good or admirable, as we have agreed in the past, or have all these former agreements been washed out during the last few days? Have we at our age failed to notice for some time that in our serious discussions we were no different from children? Above all, is the truth such as we used to say it was, whether the majority agree or not, and whether we must still suffer worse things than we do now, or will be treated more gently, that nonetheless, wrongdoing is in every way harmful and shameful to the wrongdoer? Do we say so or not?

C: We do.

S: So one must never do wrong.

C: Certainly not.

S: Nor must one, when wronged, inflict wrong in return, as the majority believe, since one must never do wrong.

C: That seems to be the case.

S: Come now, should one injure anyone or not, Crito?

C: One must never do so.

S: Well then, if one is oneself injured, is it right, as the majority say, to inflict an injury in return, or is it not?

C: It is never right.

S: Injuring people is no different from wrongdoing.

C: That is true.

S: One should never do wrong in return, nor injure any man, whatever injury one has suffered at his hands. And Crito, see that you
d   do not agree to this, contrary to your belief. For I know that only a few people hold this view or will hold it, and there is no common ground between those who hold this view and those who do not, but they inevitably despise each other's views. So then consider very carefully whether we have this view in common, and whether you agree, and let this be the basis of our deliberation, that neither to do wrong or to return a wrong is ever right, not even to injure in return for an injury received. Or do you disagree and do not share this view as a basis for dis-
e   cussion? I have held it for a long time and still hold it now, but if you think otherwise, tell me now. If, however, you stick to our former opinion, then listen to the next point.

C: I stick to it and agree with you. So say on.

S: Then I state the next point, or rather I ask you: when one has come to an agreement that is just with someone, should one fulfill it or cheat on it?

C: One should fulfill it.

S: See what follows from this: if we leave here without the city's
50   permission, are we injuring people whom we should least injure? And are we sticking to a just agreement, or not?

C: I cannot answer your question, Socrates. I do not know.

S: Look at it this way. If, as we were planning to run away from here, or whatever one should call it, the laws and the state came and confronted us and asked: "Tell me, Socrates, what are you intending to do? Do you not by this action you are attempting intend to destroy us,
b   the laws, and indeed the whole city, as far as you are concerned? Or do you think it possible for a city not to be destroyed if the verdicts of its courts have no force but are nullified and set at naught by private individuals?" What shall we answer to this and other such arguments? For many things could be said, especially by an orator on behalf of this law we are destroying, which orders that the judgments of the courts shall
c   be carried out. Shall we say in answer, "The city wronged me, and its decision was not right." Shall we say that, or what?

C: Yes, by Zeus, Socrates, that is our answer.

S: Then what if the laws said: "Was that the agreement between us, Socrates, or was it to respect the judgments that the city came to?" And if we wondered at their words, they would perhaps add: "Socrates, do not wonder at what we say but answer, since you are accustomed to proceed by question and answer. Come now, what accusation do you   d
bring against us and the city, that you should try to destroy us? Did we not, first, bring you to birth, and was it not through us that your father married your mother and begat you? Tell us, do you find anything to criticize in those of us who are concerned with marriage?" And I would say that I do not criticize them. "Or in those of us concerned with the nurture of babies and the education that you too received? Were those assigned to that subject not right to instruct your father to educate you in the arts and in physical culture?" And I would say that they were   e
right. "Very well," they would continue, "and after you were born and nurtured and educated, could you, in the first place, deny that you are our offspring and servant, both you and your forefathers? If that is so, do you think that we are on an equal footing as regards the right, and that whatever we do to you it is right for you to do to us? You were not on an equal footing with your father as regards the right, nor with your master if you had one, so as to retaliate for anything they did to you, to   51
revile them if they reviled you, to beat them if they beat you, and so with many other things. Do you think you have this right to retaliation against your country and its laws? That if we undertake to destroy you and think it right to do so, you can undertake to destroy us, as far as you can, in return? And will you say that you are right to do so, you who truly care for virtue? Is your wisdom such as not to realize that your country is to be honoured more than your mother, your father and all your ancestors, that it is more to be revered and more sacred, and that it counts for more among the gods and sensible men, that you   b
must worship it, yield to it and placate its anger more than your father's? You must either persuade it or obey its orders, and endure in silence whatever it instructs you to endure, whether blows or bonds, and if it leads you into war to be wounded or killed, you must obey. To do so is right, and one must not give way or retreat or leave one's post, but both in war and in courts and everywhere else, one must obey the commands of one's city and country, or persuade it as to the nature of   c
justice. It is impious to bring violence to bear against your mother or father, it is much more so to use it against your country." What shall we say in reply, Crito, that the laws speak the truth, or not?

C: I think they do.

S: "Reflect now, Socrates," the laws might say "that if what we say is true, you are not treating us rightly by planning to do what you are

planning. We have given you birth, nurtured you, educated you, we
d   have given you and all other citizens a share of all the good things we
could. Even so, by giving every Athenian the opportunity, after he has
reached manhood and observed the affairs of the city and us the laws,
we proclaim that if we do not please him, he can take his possessions
and go wherever he pleases. Not one of our laws raises any obstacle or
forbids him, if he is not satisfied with us or the city, if one of you wants
to go and live in a colony or wants to go anywhere else, and keep his
e   property. We say, however, that whoever of you remains, when he sees
how we conduct our trials and manage the city in other ways, has in
fact come to an agreement with us to obey our instructions. We say
that the one who disobeys does wrong in three ways, first because in us
he disobeys his parents, also those who brought him up, and because,
in spite of his agreement, he neither obeys us nor, if we do something
52   wrong, does he try to persuade us to do better. Yet we only propose
things, we do not issue savage commands to do whatever we order; we
give two alternatives, either to persuade us or to do what we say. He
does neither. We do say that you too, Socrates, are open to those
charges if you do what you have in mind; you would be among, not the
least, but the most guilty of the Athenians." And if I should say
"Why so?" they might well be right to upbraid me and say that I am
among the Athenians who most definitely came to that agreement with
b   them. They might well say: "Socrates, we have convincing proofs that
we and the city were congenial to you. You would not have dwelt here
most consistently of all the Athenians if the city had not been exceed-
ingly pleasing to you. You have never left the city, even to see a festi-
val, nor for any other reason except military service; you have never
gone to stay in any other city, as people do; you have had no desire to
c   know another city or other laws; we and our city satisfied you.
     "So decisively did you choose us and agree to be a citizen under us.
Also, you have had children in this city, thus showing that it was congenial to you. Then at your trial you could have assessed your penalty
at exile if you wished, and you are now attempting to do against the
city's wishes what you could then have done with her consent. Then
you prided yourself that you did not resent death, but you chose, as
you said, death in preference to exile. Now, however, those words do
not make you ashamed, and you pay no heed to us, the laws, as you
d   plan to destroy us, and you act like the meanest type of slave by trying
to run away, contrary to your undertakings and your agreement to live
as a citizen under us. First then, answer us on this very point, whether
we speak the truth when we say that you agreed, not only in words but
by your deeds, to live in accordance with us." What are we to say to
that, Crito? Must we not agree?

C: We must, Socrates.

S: "Surely," they might say, "you are breaking the undertakings
and agreements that you made with us without compulsion or deceit,   e
and under no pressure of time for deliberation. You have had seventy
years during which you could have gone away if you did not like us,
and if you thought our agreements unjust. You did not choose to go to   53
Sparta or to Crete, which you are always saying are well governed, nor
to any other city, Greek or foreign. You have been away from Athens
less than the lame or the blind or other handicapped people. It is clear
that the city has been outstandingly more congenial to you than to
other Athenians, and so have we, the laws, for what city can please
without laws? Will you then not now stick to our agreements? You will,
Socrates, if we can persuade you, and not make yourself a laughingstock by leaving the city.

"For consider what good you will do yourself or your friends by
breaking our agreements and committing such a wrong? It is pretty
obvious that your friends will themselves be in danger of exile, disfran-
chisement and loss of property. As for yourself, if you go to one of the   b
nearby cities — Thebes or Megara, both are well governed — you will
arrive as an enemy to their government; all who care for their city will
look on you with suspicion, as a destroyer of the laws. You will also
strengthen the conviction of the jury that they passed the right sentence
on you, for anyone who destroys the laws could easily be thought to   c
corrupt the young and the ignorant. Or will you avoid cities that are
well governed and men who are civilized? If you do this, will your life
be worth living? Will you have social intercourse with them and not be
ashamed to talk to them? And what will you say? The same as you did
here, that virtue and justice are man's most precious possession, along
with lawful behaviour and the laws? Do you not think that Socrates   d
would appear to be an unseemly kind of person? One must think so. Or
will you leave those places and go to Crito's friends in Thessaly? There
you will find the greatest license and disorder, and they may enjoy
hearing from you how absurdly you escaped from prison in some dis-
guise, in a leather jerkin or some other things in which escapees wrap
themselves, thus altering your appearance. Will there be no one to say
that you, likely to live but a short time more, were so greedy for life that
you transgressed the most important laws? Possibly, Socrates, if you do   e
not annoy anyone, but if you do, many disgraceful things will be said
about you.

"You will spend your time ingratiating yourself with all men, and
be at their beck and call. What will you do in Thessaly but feast, as if
you had gone to a banquet in Thessaly? As for those conversations of
yours about justice and the rest of virtue, where will they be? You say

54 you want to live for the sake of your children, that you may bring them up and educate them. How so? Will you bring them up and educate them by taking them to Thessaly and making strangers of them, that they may enjoy that too? Or not so, but they will be better brought up and educated here, while you are alive, though absent? Yes, your friends will look after them. Will they look after them if you go and live in Thessaly, but not if you go away to the underworld? If those who
b profess themselves your friends are any good at all, one must assume that they will.

   "Be persuaded by us who have brought you up, Socrates. Do not value either your children or your life or anything else more than goodness, in order that when you arrive in Hades you may have all this as your defence before the rulers there. If you do this deed, you will not think it better or more just or more pious here, nor will any one of your friends, nor will it be better for you when you arrive yonder. As it is, you depart, if you depart, after being wronged not by us, the laws, but
c by men; but if you depart after shamefully returning wrong for wrong and injury for injury, after breaking your agreement and contract with us, after injuring those you should injure least — yourself, your friends, your country and us — we shall be angry with you while you are still alive, and our brothers, the laws of the underworld, will not receive you kindly, knowing that you tried to destroy us as far as you could. Do not let Crito persuade you, rather than us, to do what he
d says."

   Crito, my dear friend, be assured that these are the words I seem to hear, as the Corybants seem to hear the music of their flutes, and the echo of these words resounds in me, and makes it impossible for me to hear anything else. As far as my present beliefs go, if you speak in opposition to them, you will speak in vain. However, if you think you can accomplish anything, speak.

   C: I have nothing to say, Socrates.

   S: Let it be then, Crito, and let us act in this way, since this is the
e way the god is leading us.

PHAEDO
Death Scene

In the Phaedo, *a number of Socrates' friends have come to visit him in prison on the last day of his life, as he will drink the hemlock at sundown. The main topic of their conversation is the nature of the soul and the arguments for its immortality. This takes up most of the dialogue. Then Socrates tells a rather elaborate myth on the shape of the earth in a hollow of which we live, and of which we know nothing of the splendours of its surface, the purer air and brighter heavens. The myth then deals with the dwelling places of various kinds of souls after death. The following passage immediately follows the conclusion of the myth.*

No sensible man would insist that these things are as I have described them, but I think it is fitting for a man to risk the belief — for the risk is a noble one — that this, or something like this, is true about our souls and their dwelling places, since the soul is evidently immortal, and a man should repeat this to himself as if it were an incantation, which is why I have been prolonging my tale. That is the reason why a man should be of good cheer about his own soul, if during life he has ignored the pleasures of the body and its ornamentation as of no concern to him and doing him more harm than good, but has seriously concerned himself with the pleasures of learning, and adorned his soul not with alien but with its own ornaments, namely moderation, righteousness, courage, freedom, and truth, and in that state awaits his journey to the underworld.

Now you, Simmias, Cebes, and the rest of you, Socrates continued, will each take that journey at some other time but my fated day calls me now, as a tragic character might say, and it is about time for me to have my bath, for I think it better to have it before I drink the poison and save the women the trouble of washing the corpse.

When Socrates had said this Crito spoke: Very well, Socrates, what are your instructions to me and the others about your children or any-

114d

e

115

b

55

thing else? What can we do that would please you most? — Nothing new, Crito, said Socrates, but what I am always saying, that you will please me and mine and yourselves, by taking good care of your own selves in whatever you do, even if you do not agree with me now, but if you neglect your own selves, and are unwilling to live following the

c   tracks, as it were, of what we have said now and on previous occasions, you will achieve nothing even if you strongly agree with me at this moment.

We shall be eager to follow your advice, said Crito, but how shall we bury you?

In any way you like, said Socrates, if you can catch me and I do not escape you. And laughing quietly, looking at us, he said: I do not convince Crito that I am this Socrates talking to you here and ordering all I

d   say, but he thinks that I am the thing which he will soon be looking at as a corpse, and so he asks how he shall bury me. I have been saying for some time and at some length that after I have drunk the poison I shall no longer be with you but will leave you to go and enjoy some good fortunes of the blessed, but it seems that I have said all this to him in vain in an attempt to reassure you and myself too. Give a pledge to Crito on my behalf, he said, the opposite pledge to that he gave to the jury. He pledged that I would stay, you must pledge that I will not stay after I

e   die, but that I shall go away, so that Crito will bear it more easily when he sees my body being burned or buried and will not be angry on my behalf, as if I were suffering terribly, and so that he should not say at the funeral that he is laying out, or carrying out, or burying Socrates. For know you well, my dear Crito, that to express oneself badly is not only faulty as far as the language goes, but does some harm to the soul. You must be of good cheer, and say you are burying my body, and

116   bury it in any way you like and think most customary.

After saying this he got up and went to another room to take his bath, and Crito followed him and he told us to wait for him. So we stayed, talking among ourselves, questioning what had been said, and then again talking of the great misfortune that had befallen us. We all felt as if we had lost a father and would be orphaned for the rest of our

b   lives. When he had washed, his children were brought to him — two of his sons were small and one was older — and the women of his household came to him. He spoke to them before Crito and gave them what instructions he wanted. Then he sent the women and children away, and he himself joined us. It was now close to sunset, for he had stayed inside for some time. He came and sat down after his bath and con-

c   versed for a short while, when the officer of the Eleven came and stood by him and said: "I shall not reproach you as I do the others, Socrates.

They are angry with me and curse me when, obeying the orders of my superiors, I tell them to drink the poison. During the time you have been here I have come to know you in other ways as the noblest, the gentlest, and the best man who has ever come here. So now too I know that you will not make trouble for me; you know who is responsible and you will direct your anger against them. You know what message I bring. Fare you well, and try to endure what you must as easily as possible." The officer was weeping as he turned away and went out. Socrates looked up at him and said: "Fare you well also, we shall do as you bid us." And turning to us he said: How pleasant the man is! During the whole time I have been here he has come in and conversed with me from time to time, a most agreeable man. And how genuinely he now weeps for me. Come, Crito, let us obey him. Let someone bring the poison if it is ready; if not, let the man prepare it.

But Socrates, said Crito, I think the sun still shines upon the hills and has not yet set. I know that others drink the poison quite a long time after they have received the order, eating and drinking quite a bit, and some of them enjoy intimacy with their loved ones. Do not hurry; there is still some time.

It is natural, Crito, for them to do so, said Socrates, for they think they derive some benefit from doing this, but it is not fitting for me. I do not expect any benefit from drinking the poison a little later, except to become ridiculous in my own eyes for clinging to life, and be sparing of it when there is none left. So do as I ask and do not refuse me.

Hearing this, Crito nodded to the slave who was standing near him; the slave went out and after a time came back with the man who was to administer the poison, carrying it made ready in a cup. When Socrates saw him he said: Well, my good man, you are an expert in this, what must one do? — "Just drink it and walk around until your legs feel heavy, and then lie down and it will act of itself." And he offered the cup to Socrates who took it quite cheerfully, Echecrates, without a tremor or any change of feature or colour, but looking at the man from under his eyebrows as was his wont, asked: "What do you say about pouring a libation from this drink? Is it allowed?" — "We only mix as much as we believe will suffice," said the man.

I understand, Socrates said, but one is allowed, indeed one must, utter a prayer to the gods that the journey from here to yonder may be fortunate. This is my prayer and may it be so.

And while he was saying this, he was holding the cup, and then drained it calmly and easily. Most of us had been able to hold back our tears reasonably well up till then, but when we saw him drinking it and after he drank it, we could hold them back no longer; my own tears came in floods against my will. So I covered my face. I was weeping for myself — not for him, but for my misfortune in being deprived of such

d   a comrade. Even before me, Crito was unable to restrain his tears and got up. Apollodorus had not ceased from weeping before, and at this moment his noisy tears and anger made everybody present break down, except Socrates. "What is this," he said, "you strange fellows. It is mainly for this reason that I sent the women away, to avoid such un-

e   seemliness, for I am told one should die in good omened silence. So keep quiet and control yourselves."

His words made us ashamed, and we checked our tears. He walked around, and when he said his legs were heavy he lay on his back as he had been told to do, and the man who had given him the poison touched his body, and after a while tested his feet and legs, pressed

118   hard upon his foot and asked him if he felt this, and Socrates said no. Then he pressed his calves, and made his way up his body and showed us that it was cold and stiff. He felt it himself and said that when the cold reached his heart he would be gone. As his belly was getting cold Socrates uncovered his head — he had covered it — and said — these were his last words — "Crito, we owe a cock to Asclepius;[1] make this offering to him and do not forget." — "It shall be done," said Crito, "tell us if there is anything else," but there was no answer. Shortly afterwards Socrates made a movement; the man uncovered him and his eyes were fixed. Seeing this Crito closed his mouth and his eyes.

Such was the end of our comrade, Echecrates, a man who, we would say, was of all those we have known the best, and also the wisest and the most upright.

---

1. A cock was sacrificed to Asclepius by the sick people who slept in his temples, hoping for a cure. Socrates obviously means that death is a cure for the ills of life.